ON A FAST TRACK WITH GOD

Spiritual Fitness Through Perseverance

STEPHANIE VIGNERY

Copyright © 2017 by Stephanie Vignery

On a Fast Track with God: Spiritual Fitness Through Perseverance
By Stephanie Vignery

ISBN-13: 978-1-64136-070-8

All rights reserved solely by the author. The author guarantees all contents are original and do not infringe upon the legal rights of any other person or work, and that this book is not libelous, plagiarized, or in any other way illegal. If any portion of this book is fictitious, the author guarantees it does not represent any real event or person in a way that could be deemed libelous. No part of this book may be reproduced in any form without the permission of the author.

Unless otherwise indicated, Bible quotations are taken from THE HOLY BIBLE, NEW INTERNATIONAL VERSION®, NIV® Copyright © 1973, 1978, 1984, 2011 by Biblica, Inc.®
Used by permission. All rights reserved worldwide.

Scripture quotations marked (NLT) are taken from *Holy Bible, New Living Translation,* copyright © 1996, 2004, 2015 by Tyndale House Foundation. Used by permission of Tyndale House Publishers Inc., Carol Stream, Illinois 60188. All rights reserved.

CONTENTS

Foreword – Carol Koehler — v

Starting Blocks — 1

Lap 1 – Embrace God's Plan — 3

Lap 2 – Totally Surrendered — 5

Lap 3 – Enjoy God's Presence — 8

Lap 4 – Absolutely Free — 11

Lap 5 – Start Completely Clean — 13

The Pace — 17

Lap 6 – Clear Your Mind — 19

Lap 7 – Reject Worry — 21

Lap 8 – Overcome Fear — 23

Lap 9 – Learn to Trust — 25

Lap 10 – Change Your Priorities — 27

Lap 11 – Prioritize Your Time — 29

Lap 12 – Are You Pleasing People or God? — 31

Lap 13 – Are You Letting Go and Letting God? — 33

Lap 14 – Rest in His Hands — 35

Lap 15 – God Knows You — 37

Lap 16 – You Are Enough — 39

Lap 17 – Nothing Is Impossible with God	42
Lap 18 – Receive His Peace	44
Lap 19 – Receive His Strength	46
Lap 20 – Receive His Provision	48
Lap 21 – Receive His Blessing	51
Lap 22 – Be Thankful	53
Lap 23 – Love Radically	55
Lap 24 – Develop Your Obedience	57
Lap 25 – Develop Your Faith	60
Lap 26 – Develop Generosity, Pt. 1 (The Whole Heart)	63
Lap 27 – Develop Generosity, Pt. 2 (The Tenth Part)	66
Lap 28 – Develop Gratitude	69
Lap 29 – Be Patient	72
Lap 30 – Endure Trials	74
Lap 31 – Develop Perseverance	77
Lap 32 – Be Content	80
Lap 33 – God Fulfills Our Desires	82
Lap 34 – Laugh More	85
Lap 35 – Live Joyfully	87
Home Stretch	**89**
Lap 36 – Is God Calling You?	91
Lap 37 – Waiting on God	94
Lap 38 – Right Thing at the Wrong Time	97
Lap 39 – Right Thing at the Right Time	100
Finish Line	**103**
Lap 40 – Hope and a Future	105
Acknowledgements	107

FOREWORD

Several years ago, my niece Stephanie mentioned to me that she felt God was leading her to write a devotional. I knew of her love for Jesus and her determination to follow Him, so I wasn't surprised when she let me know recently that it had been completed.

The title, "On a Fast Track with God," is actually a play on words. In the book, Stephanie refers to 18 different times when she was "on a fast with God." Fasting is something she has done consistently in her life for the last 10 to 15 years, and she has seen amazing results and answers to prayers. Many of the lessons in these devotions came as a result of her times of fasting. It has been through these wonderful times that Stephanie's faith in God has been built up to a stronger level.

Stephanie's goal with this book is to challenge us, her readers, to stay on the right track by keeping our focus on God and His Word. She uses real life experiences that each of us can relate to, and she backs them up with Scripture that can encourage us. Each of her devotions is presented as a "lap" that she runs with us. And as we run, she offers words to prepare our minds, influence our spirits, and impact our prayers. Like the good coach that she is, she reminds us to *Focus*, *Push*, and *Breathe* as we run our race.

During these 40 laps in 40 days, "Coach" Stephanie will bring back recurring themes and repeat important verses from the Bible because people in training need to hear things more than once. We need to be encouraged consistently and constantly.

Someone once said that "It is good to have a fit body. And it is better to have a fit mind controlling a fit body. But it is best to have a fit spirit leading a fit mind and body." If *you* want to come up higher in your Christian walk, Stephanie's good coaching can challenge you to make choices that will help you grow. I believe this book will become one of your favorites.

– Carol Koehler

ON A FAST TRACK WITH GOD
STARTING BLOCKS

"[I am] confident of this, that He who began a good work in you will carry it on to completion until the day of Christ Jesus"

(Philippians 1:6).

LAP 1

EMBRACE GOD'S PLAN

FOCUS: Words to Prepare Your Mind

"God has big plans for you; bigger than you can ever imagine."
- Margaret Feinberg, Imagine Devotional Journal

"'For I know the plans I have for you,' declares the Lord, 'plans to prosper you and not to harm you, plans to give you hope and a future'"
(Jeremiah 29:11).

PUSH: Words to Influence Your Spirit

Do you ever wonder what your purpose is, or what plans God has for your life, or maybe in simpler terms; what you want to be when you grow up?

I often ask myself these same kinds of questions. "Lord, what do You want me to do?" And I feel as if His answer is always "Be patient." "Be still, and know that I am God" (Psalm 46:10). "Trust in the Lord with all your heart" (Proverbs 3:5). "Cast all your anxiety on Him because He cares for you" (1 Peter 5:7). And I am often reminded of these words of Jesus; "Do not worry about tomorrow, for tomorrow will worry about itself. Each day has enough trouble of its own" (Matthew 6:34).

I don't know if you can relate to this, but I am constantly thinking of new ways to do things. You see, I have my hands in a little bit of everything. I am always looking for ways to create opportunities in my life to grow more, accomplish more, and be where I want to be. So much so that I often forget to stop and smell the roses, and just listen to what God wants to say to me.

I am too busy thinking about "what I want" or "where I need to be" in life. I often find that 'I want/I need' mode doesn't leave room for the inner peace God desires for me to have.

I have come to realize that He wants us to find perfect peace in Him first, and then, when our focus is on Him, everything else will seem to fall into place. When we let go of trying to make everything happen too fast, God's peace comes. Being at peace allows God to bring about freedom in various areas of our life. Being free makes it easier for us to do exactly what He wants us to do. Our focus should not be on working to get what we want or striving to be where we would like to be. Our priority in life is to create and build an intimate relationship with Jesus Christ. He told us to "seek first [God's] kingdom and His righteousness, and all these things [food, water, and clothing] will be given to [us] as well" (Matthew 6:33). God opens and closes the doors of our 'wants' and 'needs' when and where they should be opened and closed.

So I encourage you today to look at these things in your own life; look at them through God's eyes. Like they say; when God closes one door, He always opens another. It might not be exactly what you are expecting, but remember; God has your best interest in mind. When I look back on my life, I see that He has never failed me. He has always been there when I needed Him. And things have always happened in God's perfect timing. So, if you are searching for what you should be doing in your life, wait patiently and listen—as difficult as that may seem to be. God's plan is the best plan, and He knows the exact right thing you need at the right time. His timing is always perfect.

BREATHE: Words to Impact Your Prayers

Acknowledge and Admit:

Lord, You are my leader and my guide.

I am not always aware of Your plan for my life.

Appreciate and Ask:

Thank You for opening and closing doors according to Your will.

I ask You to help me be patient; help me see and know Your plans for me.

LAP 2

TOTALLY SURRENDERED

FOCUS: Words to Prepare Your Mind

*"When you throw yourself at the foot of God's throne,
He mercifully gives you the grace to remain strong and true."*

- Sheila Walsh, Imagine Devotional Journal

"We have [a high priest—Jesus the Son of God] who has been tempted in every way, just as we are—yet He did not sin. Let us then approach God's throne of grace with confidence, so that we may receive mercy and find grace to help us in our time of need"

(Hebrews 4:15-16).

PUSH: Words to Influence Your Spirit

Have you ever gotten to the point in life where you just want to drop everything you're doing and say, "I just can't take it anymore . . . I'm done . . . I give up"?

If we are honest with ourselves, haven't we all done this at one time or another? When we get to that point, it feels as though we're all alone. When we have given up, we believe that no one else in the world feels the way we do. Right? When we are in a dark place mentally, it is much harder to handle things on our own, especially if we're battling addiction, dealing with a very challenging child, facing a divorce or the death of a loved one, or something else along those lines.

Whatever it might be—no matter *when* it happens in our life—let me share this precious truth with you now: You don't have to live your life in isolation.

You are never alone. God is always right there with you, with His arms wide open. From the Bible, He says to us, "Come to Me, all you who are weary and burdened, and I will give you rest" (Matthew 11:28).

Satan knows our areas of weakness. He knows how to get the best of us and defeat us. However, the Bible says, "Submit yourselves, then, to God. Resist the devil, and he will flee from you" (James 4:7). Our pastor once said, "The true meaning of surrendering (or submitting yourself to God) is just inviting the Spirit of God into every part of your life at every moment." This statement might challenge you; I struggle with it on a daily basis. For some reason, I like to hold on to things or control things around me, or at least I try to. Every time I do, I find that I am only making myself miserable. I take on added stress and worry when there is no need to. However, when I choose to lay things at Jesus' feet, He takes away my worries and fears. I have found that when I make that choice—*Wow!*—the peace that comes over me is so freeing!

It was while I was on a fast with God that our pastor was talking about surrendering ourselves to the Lord. During that Sunday service, something powerful happened to me in regard to an area I had struggled with for quite a while. It was in the area of "performance"—doing things in hopes that others would approve of me and my efforts. I knew that morning that God was inviting me to surrender my performance mentality to Him. I realized that I don't have to work hard to be good enough in everything I do. I don't have to prove anything to anybody! All I have to do is be "me." That is enough. That day, I prayed a prayer of surrender and took on a new mentality. I stood up to receive freedom from everything that held me back from being all that God created me to be. It was quite a moment!

You know, if you think about it, none of us is too concerned with how next person "performs" anyway. Honestly, many people in the world are only looking out for number one—themselves. Here's what I have found; there is only one who cares about our performance—and it's not even the performance part that He looks at, it's our heart. The God who cares is the God who says, "Come to Me, . . . and I will give you rest" (Matthew 11:28).

So I encourage you today to ask yourself; "Who am I trying to please? Is it God? Or am I trying to please those around me?" I've had to answer that one myself. It's like preacher and author John Ortberg once said; "The most important task in your life is not what you do, but whom you become."

BREATHE: Words to Impact Your Prayers

Acknowledge and Admit:

Lord, You are the source of true rest,
the One who invites me to come to You.

I strive to control things and care too
much about what others think of me.

Appreciate and Ask:

Thank You for offering Your peace in place of my chaos.

I ask You to help me surrender to You and Your will.

LAP 3

ENJOY GOD'S PRESENCE

FOCUS: Words to Prepare Your Mind

"God can't give us peace and happiness apart from Himself because there is no such thing."

- C.S. Lewis, Mere Christianity

"No one will be able to stand against you all the days of your life. As I was with Moses, so I will be with you; I will never leave you nor forsake you"

(Joshua 1:5).

PUSH: Words to Influence Your Spirit

Did you know that God is always with you and that you can experience His presence?

When we feel Him close to us, it is the most wonderful feeling there is. There are certainly times when we feel God's presence more strongly than we do at other times. But for me; I get goosebumps all over, and it seems like my emotions are much more intense. I cannot help but tear up when I feel God's peace come over me. Whether you have felt God's presence like this or not, I want to give you hope today that He is right there beside you with open arms. He wants to walk with you every step of your life.

Sometimes, we might not hear God, or see Him, or allow Him into our lives, and so we don't experience the love that we desire—the love He desires to express to us.

I remember a time in my life when I felt that God was especially near to me. It was while I was on one of my 40-day fasts with Him. I was journaling about my day. As I wrote, it was literally as if I began to see my thoughts spelled out on the paper before I had even considered them in my mind. However, they were not my thoughts. It was awesome and yet scary at the same time; almost an out-of-body experience. Have you ever had a moment like this? I remember God telling me so clearly through those written words to "let go" of something I had been holding tightly to. He invited me to "trust Him completely." I knew He would take care of my family and me.

A few days went by, and without noticing it, my pride, my lack of trust and faith, or whatever you might call it, came creeping back in. I had "let go"—so I thought—but I guess it was in my own way. I was not trusting Him completely like He had asked me to. Because I wasn't clearly aware of it, I didn't really do what I needed to. I have to admit this honestly; that period of my life was one of the most miserable I had had in a long time.

So I encourage you today to look for ways and opportunities to experience God's presence. However, I have to tell you; if He asks you to do something during that time, you need to do it. Don't do it halfway like I did.

On the other hand, if you feel as though you may have missed God by not listening or doing what He has asked of you in the past, don't get discouraged and beat yourself up about it. God is a forgiving and ever-loving God who is faithful to us whether or not we are faithful to Him. Isn't that liberating to know?

I see my story now as a learning experience. I know that when God asks something of me, I am going to follow His leading. I find that I am much more open to what God is saying and I am doing my best to be obedient to Him. Through it all, I have seen some awesome blessings come into my life and my family's. That doesn't mean I don't struggle from time to time with knowing when God is speaking to me. However, I believe that He also gives me peace when He is speaking to me. He opens and closes the doors in my life.

Remember; He will not put you in a position that will harm you. You can trust Him completely because He knows what the very best for you is. You can never go wrong listening to God.

BREATHE: Words to Impact Your Prayers

Acknowledge and Admit:

Lord, You are with me and available to me all the time.

I am not always aware of Your presence.

Appreciate and Ask:

Thank You for being faithful, even when I am not.

I ask You to help me know You better and feel Your presence more and more.

LAP 4

ABSOLUTELY FREE

FOCUS: Words to Prepare Your Mind

"I have learned that life is exceedingly difficult and that God is amazingly big. He will reign over our greatest losses, rectify our worst failures, and remedy our deepest insecurities."

- Patsy Clairmont, Imagine Devotional Journal

"Jesus said to the people who believed in Him, 'You are truly My disciples if you remain faithful to My teachings. And you will know the truth, and the truth will set you free'"

(John 8:31-32 NLT).

PUSH: Words to Influence Your Spirit

Have you ever really thought about emotional and personal freedom, and the areas and ways you would like to experience more of it in your life?

Freedom doesn't only mean 'getting rid of sin and strongholds in our life,' although those things certainly hold us back from having the personal, intimate relationship God desires for us to have with Him. Having freedom in our life means that we realize who God created and redeemed us to be, and we are living that life.

Jesus identified Satan as "the thief [who] comes only to steal and kill and destroy" (John 10:10). The devil wants to do everything in his power to keep us from experiencing the freedom we desire to have in our lives. He lies to us over and over again until we start believing those lies. When we hear something enough, we begin believing that it is the truth, even when it is not. When we allow our enemy to have the power to control our lives in this way, it is an open door for him to steal our joy, kill our dreams, and destroy our trust in God.

Satan's strongest grip on us is in the areas where we struggle the most. He focuses our attention on those struggles and makes the temptation even more enticing through his lies, often even getting us to justify our sins. Satan's greatest way to hurt us is by keeping our focus on these areas of weakness. That is why it is so important to live in God's presence at all times. I have found that great things happen in God's presence. Being close to Him is what defeats our fears and brings light to our dark places—our struggles. I don't know about you, but when I experience God's presence, the feeling of freedom and joy that happens is so strong that I just want to stay near Him forever.

So I encourage you today; if you truly want freedom in your life, the best way to find it is by being in God's presence. Take time intentionally to be with Him on a daily basis, reading the Bible and praying. Be quiet and still. Ask Him to speak to you and anticipate hearing His voice. More than this, when He does speak to you, don't just *hear* what He says but *listen and receive* it. Take it personally.

Remember; Jesus died on the cross so we can live a life of abundance and freedom. So I say to you now; choose to be free in Christ! Since our life revolves around the things we seek. Seek Him today!

BREATHE: Words to Impact Your Prayers

Acknowledge and Admit:

Lord, You are the God who can set me free from sin and bondage.

I tend to be deceived by the enemy and believe things that are not true.

Appreciate and Ask:

Thank You for not allowing Satan to get the best of me.

I ask You to teach me Your truth and help me believe it.

LAP 5

START COMPLETELY CLEAN

FOCUS: Words to Prepare Your Mind

"It's okay if I'm damaged by life's adversities; I can still stand strong because the Lord makes his strength known in our weakness."

– **Patsy Clairmont, Imagine Devotional Journal**

"Create in me a pure heart, O God, and renew a steadfast spirit within me. Do not cast me from Your presence or take Your Holy Spirit from me. Restore to me the joy of Your salvation and grant me a willing spirit, to sustain me"

(Psalm 51:10-12).

PUSH: Words to Influence Your Spirit

Have you ever felt so excited about something that happened to you that you felt you just had to go and tell everyone? And no matter what, nothing was going to bring you down or stand in the way of your happiness and joy?

Well, here's a story of mine like that.

While I was on a fast with God, He put an interesting opportunity in front of me. My first thought was; *Well, this might be helpful. I could probably benefit from it.* This particular opportunity was not just any ordinary, everyday opportunity though. It was a chance to experience physical, mental, emotional, and spiritual cleansing during a 6-day retreat with some ladies from my church. Have you ever had an opportunity like that?

When the opportunity was presented to me, I was a little nervous to disclose some of *my stuff* to the other women. But I knew that if I acknowledged at least some of my junk, I could begin healing from it.

I thought, Well, I am always asking God to cleanse me and forgive my sins. Maybe this is something I <u>need</u> to do.

I decided to go, and let me tell you, it was one of the most vulnerable yet powerful and rewarding experiences I have ever had.

I laid everything out before my Christian sisters during that week; my sins and my fears, as well as experiences from my past which I thought I had dealt with. I know I had dealt with them to a certain degree before this, but I had never released them before others by confessing them out loud. Let me tell you; there is real power in the act of releasing things out loud. Things came up that I had stuffed down inside me. I did not realize I had never released them before. Some of those things, I know now, were keeping me from having a fully intimate relationship with Christ. It felt like I received freedom from the bondage of all my sins. Dealing with issues like this, surrounded by sisters who cared about my freedom in Christ, was also freeing, yet scary too. However, I know, without a shadow of a doubt, that God has completely forgiven me for things in my past. I also know that I have forgiven myself too—that is a key thing to do. Sometimes, it is easier to believe that God has forgiven us than it is to forgive ourselves for the very same things.

I share this experience with you—with all of its "I just have to go tell somebody" emotion—because God is *so good* all of the time. If there is anything holding you back, any bondage of sin you need to be free from, I encourage you today to not wait. Do something like this as soon as you can. Let everything go. Confess it to God, and maybe even to others (people who care about your relationship with Him). He already knows what you are dealing with, so there is nothing to hide. God is excited for you to be free from anything which holds you back from having a truly authentic relationship with Him. He is excited not only for your relationship with Him but also to bless you in the areas in which you may have blocked Him out with sin and fear and doubt.

I promise you; when you confess your sins and ask God to forgive you, there is an amazing healing process that begins to take place. He will cleanse you from the inside out. Are you ready to start receiving the freedom and the blessings which God wants for you and your life? There's the starting gun. Do it *now*! You won't regret it.

BREATHE: Words to Impact Your Prayers

Acknowledge and Admit:

Lord, You are the One who has done everything necessary for me to be rescued.

There is darkness in my past, and brokenness deep inside me.

Appreciate and Ask:

Thank You for dying on the cross to forgive my sins, and rising from the dead so I could have new life.

I ask You to reveal anything that may be holding me back from You and cleanse me completely.

ON A FAST TRACK WITH GOD

THE PACE

"One thing I do: Forgetting what is behind and straining toward what is ahead, I press on toward the goal to win the prize for which God has called me heavenward in Christ Jesus"

(Philippians 3:13-14).

LAP 6

CLEAR YOUR MIND

FOCUS: Words to Prepare Your Mind

"Nothing is impossible with God. Nothing! Impossibility lies only in our minds, not in God's ways and means."

- Luci Swindoll, Imagine Devotional Journal

"Don't copy the behavior and customs of this world, but let God transform you into a new person by changing the way you think. Then you will learn to know God's will for you, which is good and pleasing and perfect"

(Romans 12:2 NLT).

PUSH: Words to Influence Your Spirit

Do you sometimes feel weighed down, even paralyzed, by the clutter in your mind?

Maybe, like me, you feel like there are too many things to do and too little time to do them all. Guess what. This is a symptom of being human. You and I are not the only ones who have ever felt this way. They tell us that everyone has the same amount of time each day. The key is how we manage it. How will we spend the minutes we have been given?

I am realizing more and more that staring at the petty tasks in front of me and trying to figure out how to get them all done at the same time often takes longer than just jumping in and doing them, regardless of the perfect order. If you're anything like me, then I want to give you this tip; instead of trying to do everything at once, choose the most important and dive in. Just having clarity, and a plan of action, for what I need to do puts my mind at ease. Once my mind is clear, I am able to do the task at hand—then the next one, then the next one—in a way that is more effective than rushing through all of it with the feeling that my life is in complete chaos.

Every time I stress about the stuff I haven't done yet, it takes away from feeling God's peace in my life. It negatively affects the time God desires for me to have with Him. Our ultimate purpose is to live close to God. This takes keeping our minds free of clutter so we can hear what God is telling us and be open to everything He has in mind for us. When we keep our minds free of clutter and continually seek closeness with God throughout the day, we find that His presence brings even greater order to our thoughts, as well as peace to our entire being.

So I encourage you today; choose the most important thing and do it. Don't worry about what is not getting done. And more than this, "commit to the Lord whatever you do, and He will establish your plans" (Proverbs 16:3). Continually seek closeness with God; the rest will follow.

BREATHE: Words to Impact Your Prayers

Acknowledge and Admit:

Lord, You are my highest priority.

Sometimes, my mind is cluttered with too much to do rather than the most important thing.

Appreciate and Ask:

Thank You for offering me Your peace, which brings about order.

I ask You to clear my mind of clutter and purify my heart.

LAP 7

REJECT WORRY

FOCUS: Words to Prepare Your Mind

"God wants us to live fully . . . and well. It is part of His dream for us."
- Luci Swindoll, Imagine Devotional Journal

"Therefore do not worry about tomorrow, for tomorrow will worry about itself. Each day has enough trouble of its own"
(Matthew 6:34).

PUSH: Words to Influence Your Spirit

Are you worried about anything in your life today?

If so, just stop. Take a deep breath. And say a prayer to Jesus.

Did you know that God is all around you? He promises His people that He "will be with you; He will never leave you nor forsake you" (Deuteronomy 31:8). Jesus promised, "I am with you always" (Matthew 28:20). Despite these wonderful promises, many things can hinder and block our awareness of God's presence. And one of the major things that gets in our way is worry.

In her book *Jesus Calling*, Sara Young asks us to consider something. "Who is in charge of your life? And if it is you, then you have a good reason to worry." Worry is unnecessary. When we start to feel anxious about something, we need to go back to God and ask Him to help redirect our focus. Sara also says, "God will either take care of the problem Himself or show you how to handle it."

It is easy to remember that, in this world, we will have problems. Just look around. However, we need to not to lose sight of God in our problems. He has never failed us before; why do we think He might fail us now? Our attitude rises and falls on what we choose to focus on. If we choose the world's perspective, we will worry and be anxious. If we choose God and His perspective, we will find peace.

While I was recently on a fast with God, I found myself bouncing back and forth between worry and peace regarding work-related things. It was pretty obvious that Satan was in "attack Stephanie" mode. This commonly happens when I am on a fast. It always seems to be that the closer I am to God the more Satan tries to bring me down. When we choose to fast, we have to be prepared for Satan to attack us. But remember; there is no reason to be afraid "because He who is in [us] is greater than he who is in the world" (1 John 4:4). Besides, I have found that, while I am on a fast with God, some of the most beautiful moments and blessings happen. Often during these times, God reaffirms that He is present with me. There are times when He has done this through the fact that what I read in my quiet time was just what I needed to hear. He has reaffirmed His presence through simple but profound things my children have said. And He has done it through the blessing that comes from answered prayer. It is important to have 'faith-builder' moments like that when Satan comes to tempt us to worry.

Do you remember Richard Carlson's book several years back called *Don't Sweat the Small Stuff*? Well, I encourage you today to take that advice. Stop worrying about the small stuff—as difficult as that might seem at times. Apply the "don't sweat the small stuff" principle to your life because God has everything under control. It only creates more stress and worries when you think you have to be the one in control. Remember; because God truly is in control, you can redirect your focus and know that God will either take care of your problems or show you how to handle them.

BREATHE: Words to Impact Your Prayers

Acknowledge and Admit:

Lord, You are loving and trustworthy and in complete control.

I tend to worry and find it difficult to trust You with all my heart.

Appreciate and Ask:

Thank You for always being faithful in your love for me.

*I ask You to help me keep my focus on You,
and be confident that You will take care of me.*

LAP 8

OVERCOME FEAR

FOCUS: Words to Prepare Your Mind

"The human heart quests for satisfaction and keeps at it until it finds some kind of peace in God."

- Luci Swindoll, Imagine Devotional Journal

"Do not fear, for I am with you; do not be dismayed, for I am your God. I will strengthen you and help you; I will uphold you with my righteous right hand"

(Isaiah 41:10).

PUSH: Words to Influence Your Spirit

Does fear often cloud your thinking and rule your decisions? Are you living your life from a position of fear?

If you are, then here's one word for you: *don't!*

When we live in fear, we are basically saying to God, "I don't trust You." Instead of allowing fear to steal away our joy and confidence, we need to think about the things that God has done for us. We need to remember the faith-builders He has brought into our lives to teach us His lessons. When we think of the various the ways God has shown Himself faithful in our life, peace will fill our heart and mind. We remember His words; "Do not fear, for I am with you; . . . I will strengthen you and help you" (Isaiah 41:10).

So I encourage you today to consider the faithfulness of God. You can read about it all through the Bible. You can hear it in the stories of those who have lived before us and those who live around us now. God wants to comfort you, and let you know how much He loves you and wants to take care of you. Satan, on the other hand, "comes only to steal and kill and destroy" (John 10:10). He wants to take away your joy and cause you to live in complete fear. But you don't have to. You have a choice. "The Spirit God gave us does not make us timid, but gives us power, love, and self-discipline" (2 Timothy 1:7). When you start to feel afraid, start praying. Bind the fear in the name of Jesus, and ask Him to help you let it go. I have found that, when I do this, His peace comes over me. Because He is faithful, I know He will do the same for you. He wants to give you His peace. All you have to do is let Him.

BREATHE: Words to Impact Your Prayers

Acknowledge and Admit:

Lord, You are the Prince of Peace; the One who drives away my fear.

I tend to allow doubt and fear to determine how I live.

Appreciate and Ask:

*Thank You for giving me Your Holy Spirit,
who fills me with power, love, and self-discipline.*

I ask You to set me free from my fear and give me confidence in You.

LAP 9

LEARN TO TRUST

FOCUS: Words to Prepare Your Mind

"Surrender is best demonstrated in obedience and trust."
- Rick Warren, The Purpose Driven Life

"Trust in the Lord with all your heart and lean not on your own understanding; in all your ways submit to Him, and He will make your paths straight"
(Proverbs 3:5-6).

PUSH: Words to Influence Your Spirit

Do you have a difficult time trusting?

There are times when trusting is hard for me.

Someone once told me that the way we view our earthly father has a strong influence on how we view our heavenly Father. If we feel that we have been let down by our dad, we can approach God as though we need to protect ourselves from getting hurt. Honestly, although I feel like I trust God, when it comes right down to it, I can have a difficult time with it.

I don't know if you can relate to this, but I like to have everything in my life in its place. My life is planned out, and the goals I want to reach are always right in front of me. There is nothing wrong with this—up to a point. However, I have found that, when life goes in a different direction than what I had planned, I struggle. And that means I need to stop and refocus on the right things, trusting that God has a bigger and better plan for me. For some reason, I don't do so well with that. You see, I like to do things myself and my way. I know that, when I am the one to do it, it will get done exactly the way I want it to be done. But things don't always go our way, do they?

I believe that God wants to step into our lives—often—and bring us back to reality. I can imagine Him saying, "Don't you see that what you are doing is not working, Stephanie?" I find that, when I finally let go and let God, the peace that comes over me is truly amazing.

So I encourage you today to remember that you are not alone. God sees the bigger picture of your life, and He knows what is best for you. Don't do what I have done. God is waiting with open arms, saying to you (and to me), "Trust Me." You will be amazed at what God will do when you let go.

BREATHE: Words to Impact Your Prayers

Acknowledge and Admit:

Lord, You are faithful and trustworthy.

People have failed me, and I have failed others.

Appreciate and Ask:

Thank You for having the very best in mind for me.

I ask You to help me trust You in everything I do.

LAP 10

CHANGE YOUR PRIORITIES

FOCUS: Words to Prepare Your Mind

"If we don't learn to live fully in the present much of life passes us by, lost in cobwebs of time forever."

- Luci Swindoll, Imagine Devotional Journal

"Where your treasure is, there your heart will be also"

(Matthew 6:21).

PUSH: Words to Influence Your Spirit

Do you ever wonder what kind of life you're creating? What is most important to you? What priorities are you living for? Could it be money or your work? Is it your family? Is it God?

Although I engage in this kind of self-talk on a regular basis, it is probably the most challenging. I am the mom of two little ones who need my attention constantly. I work a job or two to help make ends meet. I always set goals and work hard. I persevere until I have accomplished exactly what I want to accomplish. Determination is one of the gifts that God has given me. It is a great quality to have. Yet, the drawback for me is that, while I am pursuing my goals, I have a tendency to lose focus on things around me. And who suffers from this? My family, of course. My husband and kids get less of my attention when I am obsessing and stressing myself out trying to keep other things under control. And more than this, I think God suffers.

Someone once told me that a strength overused can become a weakness. When I find myself in the position of "over using my own strength"—over and over again—I can imagine God saying, "Stephanie, stop trying to control everything. Aren't you tired yet?"

Do you know anyone like this? Can you relate?

When I remember that I am creating a life, it really gets me to thinking, "What kind of legacy am I passing on to my children? What kind of example am I to those around me?" You see, when I allow my flesh or worldly ways to take control, I get selfish and dependent on my own resources and strength. But when God brings my attention back to Him, and I realize what kind of life I have been creating, my heart just breaks. One thing I know is that God always brings me back to my heart because it's there that I know the right thing to do.

Do I ever intentionally want to create a selfish life? Of course not. When I am leading God's way and allowing Him to be in control my life, complete peace comes over me, and a feeling of freedom surrounds me.

So I encourage you today; don't do the selfish things I have done. If you do find yourself going down that path, stop and take a second look at your motives. Allow God to be number one. You will find more fulfillment in your life than you could ever imagine. And when you let go and let God, the peace that will come over you will be amazing. Remember; it is not necessarily the result that matters, it's the adventure you've been on along the way. Stay focused on the most important things in your life. Ask yourself, "When I go home to be with Jesus, what will they say the priority in my life was; the earthly possessions I strived to get, or the people who were close to me?"

One of my friends told me something that I will always remember. "If your priorities are not aligning with your values, mission, and vision for your life, then peace will not be there, and it will continue to stir up your heart." Ask yourself again; "Where is my heart? What are my priorities?"

BREATHE: Words to Impact Your Prayers

Acknowledge and Admit:

Lord, You are much more important than the blessings You give me.

I tend to lose track of what my priorities are and what they should be.

Appreciate and Ask:

*Thank You for the relationships I have,
especially my relationship with You.*

*I ask You to make a difference in my heart so
I can make a difference in the lives of others.*

LAP 11

PRIORITIZE YOUR TIME

FOCUS: Words to Prepare Your Mind

"This day is yours. This is your time to do, to be, to accomplish, to fulfill your reason for living."

- Jan Silvious, Imagine Devotional Journal

"Encourage one another daily, as long as it is called "Today," so that none of you may be hardened by sin's deceitfulness"

(Hebrews 3:13).

PUSH: Words to Influence Your Spirit

What do you spend your time and energy on? How many hours do you put into your job and hobbies? How many minutes do you spend with friends, family, and God? How much of your time is wasted?

I'm sure you've heard the saying "Life is too short to waste. Make every day count." God wants our time. In her *Jesus Calling* devotional, Sarah Young states that "time with Him cannot be rushed because, when we are in a hurry, our mind flitters back and forth between Him and tasks ahead of us. We should push back the demands pressing in on us and create a safe place around us, a haven in which we can rest in God. He desires this time of focused attention, and He uses it to bless us, strengthening and equipping us for the days ahead. Spending time with God is a wise investment. Bring God the sacrifice of our precious time. This creates sacred space around us; space permeated with God's presence and peace."

When I first read those words, it truly opened my eyes to how precious my time with God is. We cannot hurry through our devotional time because we might miss what He is saying to us or wanting to show us about our lives. I found that time with God is vitally important in my life through the discipline of fasting. It helps me to see His blessings much more clearly. Not only that, but I also believe that my mind is much clearer. God provides the answers to my prayers. And I feel His peace more strongly, which is simply indescribable.

So I encourage you today to make the most of your time with God and focus on what He is trying to teach you. Keep your heart and mind open to what He has for you. After all, we don't want to miss out on the blessings God has for us. I truly believe that if you want clarity, if you want blessings and all that God has in store for you, you will find that spending time with God on a daily basis is exactly what you need.

BREATHE: Words to Impact Your Prayers

Acknowledge and Admit:

Lord, You are the most important person I can spend time with.

I tend to give my best time and attention to lesser things.

Appreciate and Ask:

Thank You for all of the minutes of all of the days that You give me.

I ask You to help me spend my time wisely and carefully.

LAP 12

ARE YOU PLEASING PEOPLE OR GOD?

FOCUS: Words to Prepare Your Mind

"Listen closely to your longings. God is the only one big enough to hold our longings."

- Nicole Johnson, Imagine Devotional Journal

"Trust in the Lord and do good; dwell in the land and enjoy safe pasture. Take delight in the Lord, and he will give you the desires of your heart"

(Psalm 37:3-4).

PUSH: Words to Influence Your Spirit

Have you figured out yet that you cannot please everyone?

We can try and try to please others, but we will continue to feel let down. It is an impossible task, and the end result is that we feel miserable. However, if we tried as hard to please God as we do people, we might actually see a different result; like a more fulfilling and joyful life. I would rather feel the lasting joy that I receive from pleasing God than the constant empty feeling of being let down when I try and fail to please everyone else.

I have accepted the fact that people are people, and we cannot hope to control anyone other than ourselves. I am not saying that we don't give others our best. But we treat them well because we want to, not because we might get something out of it for ourselves. We should do everything because we have a generous, giving heart, not because we feel obligated. I have found that when I do things out of obligation and false expectations, I seem to fail every time. So let's give because we want to, not because we have to.

I have also found that pleasing God gives us the results that we desire; results like love, joy, and peace. When our desire to please God is stronger than our effort to be a people-pleaser, the results are rewarding. And pleasing God is not a hard thing to do. We don't have to figure out how to please Him through our own good deeds. The beautiful this is that what pleases God is being in a personal relationship with Him, having a heart that is open and obedient to all He has for us, and living in the example of Jesus. What pleases Him is faith, "because anyone who comes to Him must believe that He exists and that He rewards those who earnestly seek Him" (Hebrews 1:6). When we are pleasing to Him, the door is wide-open for Him to use us in mighty ways. God is then free to give us the desires of our heart.

So I encourage you today; make it your intention to please God rather than people. Pleasing people will only bring you frustration and heartache because they will too often let you down, but God never will. Pleasing God will produce in you a joy that lasts. So "commit your way to the Lord; trust in Him and He will do this" (Psalm 37:5).

BREATHE: Words to Impact Your Prayers

Acknowledge and Admit:

Lord, You are faithful and true.

I can let others down as easy as they let me down.

Appreciate and Ask:

Thank You for being pleased by my faith.

I ask You to increase my faith so I can please You more, and be a blessing to others as well.

LAP 13

ARE YOU LETTING GO AND LETTING GOD?

FOCUS: Words to Prepare Your Mind

"I pray hard, work hard, and leave the rest to God."

- Florence Griffith Joyner, Hugs: Daily Inspirations for Women

"Do not be anxious about anything, but in every situation, by prayer and petition, with thanksgiving, present your requests to God. And the peace of God, which transcends all understanding, will guard your hearts and your minds in Christ Jesus"

(Philippians 4:6-7).

PUSH: Words to Influence Your Spirit

Do you have a difficult time letting go of certain situations and people and just letting God be in control of every circumstance in your life?

I went on a 25-day fast with God one January. Our whole church was fasting for the New Year. It was one of the most rewarding fasts I had ever been on to the point. God gave me a word that He wanted me to live by for that year. The word was *open-minded*.

After my fast was over, I was able to reflect on my experience. I can look back now, and see why He had me live by that word. It was a stretch for me. I have always had such a hard time letting go of control and letting God have complete control of my life. I knew He wanted me to be open to whatever it was that He had for me that year. During that time, God made me aware of something I struggle with on a regular basis. I would *think* I was letting go of things in my life, but I would soon find that I still hold on to this or that and not let God have complete control. So, in other words, I would turn over just a little bit of control. I would still keep God at arm's length and not let Him have *complete* control. Obviously, it wasn't working. So when God laid it on my heart to be open-minded, I was to let go of the controls and let Him completely guide me. I was to be open to whatever He wanted me to do and not just focus on what I wanted like I had in years past.

When I allowed God to have complete control of my heart and circumstances that year, it was the most peaceful feeling I had felt in a long time. Now there were times, of course, when it was challenging (and it still can be), however, each time I was tempted to take back the controls, God brought me back to the word *open-minded*. When He did, it forced me to look at my *why*. When I remembered *why* God was leading me on this journey of being open-minded, I experienced a new level of peace. Not only did I feel more peace in my life but my business improved, I felt a stronger bond with my family and friends, and most importantly, I felt more closely connected to my heavenly Father. I had desired for a long time to feel authentically close to Him. As I continued to let go and let God, I felt that He was hearing me when I talked to Him, and I was clearer on what He was saying to me. I am a firm believer that when we are open-minded and obedient to what God tells us, everything is clearer and things just seem to fall into place. It is an amazing thing.

So I encourage you today to stop carrying the full weight of your life and allow God to do what He wants to do. (I believe we can get in the way of what God has for us when we don't let go.) His plans are far greater than you could ever imagine. You will be surprised by what He has in store for you. Jesus is waiting with open arms, saying, "Come to Me, all you who are weary and burdened, and I will give you rest. Take My yoke upon you and learn from Me, for I am gentle and humble in heart, and you will find rest for your souls. For My yoke is easy and my burden is light" (Matthew 11:28–30). So don't wait. Let go and let God.

BREATHE: Words to Impact Your Prayers

Acknowledge and Admit:

Lord, You are the One who has my best interests at heart all of the time.

Sometimes, I think I know what is best for my life.

Appreciate and Ask:

Thank You for offering me rest for my soul.

I ask You to help me let go of the controls of my life and let You take over completely.

LAP 14

REST IN HIS HANDS

FOCUS: Words to Prepare Your Mind

"God will never let you sink under your circumstances. He always provides a safety net, and His love always encircles."

- Barbara Johnson, Hugs: Daily Inspirations for Women

"We know that in all things God works for the good of those who love Him, who have been called according to His purpose"
(Romans 8:28).

PUSH: Words to Influence Your Spirit

Do you have a difficult time resting and relaxing in the fact that you have placed the details of your life in God's hands?

I want to tell you today that our God is a limitless God. If you have a tendency to put Him in a box and limit what He can do, don't. You might be pleasantly surprised at what God can and will do if you let Him. Remember; He is for you, not against you. He wants to bless you and be right by your side. It is up to you on how closely you will allow Him to work in your life. *You choose.* Our pastor says that God will only be as close to you as you want Him to be.

At night, my son is so precious. When he wants my husband or me to lay down next to him, he will tap his hand on the bed right where he wants us to be. Then, he will put his hand on top of ours just to have the comfort of knowing we are there. I see that God works a lot like that. He continues to place His hand on us to let us know that He is there protecting and comforting us through every situation of our life. Whether we are holding His hand or not, God is still holding ours.

So I encourage you today to *not* limit God in what He can do in your life. His hand is always on you, protecting and comforting you. I can see this is true for me when I look back and see all the blessings God has given. He always provided when I was in need and never allowed me to go without. He has never failed me. Of course, that doesn't mean that there weren't rocky times when I wandered in life, but I have always gotten through those times. I am still okay. God has never failed me. I am stronger now than when I started. If there is one thing I want you to hear today, it is this; when you leave things in God's hands, there is *no* limit to what He can do.

BREATHE: Words to Impact Your Prayers

Acknowledge and Admit:

*Lord, You are the God whose hand is on my life,
protecting me and comforting me.*

I am just a child who needs to feel my heavenly Father's hand in mine.

Appreciate and Ask:

Thank You for being unlimited in Your love and power toward me.

*I ask You to help me trust that there is no limit
to what You can do in my life.*

LAP 15

GOD KNOWS YOU

FOCUS: Words to Prepare Your Mind

"God gave you an imagination so that you could join your heart with His and just see what He might do with and through you—just imagine that!"

- Sheila Walsh, Imagine Devotional Journal

*"In their hearts humans plan their course,
but the Lord establishes their steps"*

(Proverbs 16:9).

PUSH: Words to Influence Your Spirit

Do you know that God already knows everything about you, including the future and your potential in it?

God knew everything about us before anything ever happened. As we live for Him, He prepares us for the details of His plan for our lives. Obviously, we don't know what lies ahead for us. And when bad things happen unexpectedly, even then, God can turn the circumstance around for us. "We know that in all things God works for the good of those who love Him, who have been called according to His purpose" (Romans 8:28).

God knows our heart and our desires. I believe He actually puts good desires in our heart, and He Himself wants to bring them about. But sometimes, I think He also allows the desires we have that don't line up with His plan to take place. I know I have learned, by experience, about the differences between my own will and His. And in a number of situations, God protected me from what I thought I wanted. I look back on it all now and see why God did not want certain things in my life, so I am thankful they did not come about. God had greater plans for me. He also has great plans for you, too.

I believe that God plants seeds like skills and talents, dreams and innovations, career paths and relationships, families and missions in our hearts, then He invites us to follow Him into the fulfillment of those things. God knows our heart, and He wants to give us the desires of our heart.

Often, we discover our heart's desire way before we are ready for the fulfillment. God wants to teach us and mold us before He allows us to have those desires. What I have found in my life is that every good thing from God happens in His timing. God sees what is ahead of us, and He gives us those desires when He knows we're ready. But no matter what, in everything we do, whether we have our desires or not, God wants us to praise Him and give Him glory.

So I encourage you today; if you have a desire (or even a need) that you want to see fulfilled, rest assured, God already knows what is best for us and how to take you there. He already knows the outcome. So look at your desires. If they have not been met yet, maybe it is not God's timing. Maybe you should take on a new perspective. Take time to reflect on where you are and praise God for whatever it is that He has given you at this point.

Just remember; God gave you your desires for a reason. In His timing and at His leading, everything will come together in the way He intends. Don't settle for anything less. Continue to thank Him in all circumstances. The Bible says that God's plans are "to prosper you and not to harm you, plans to give you hope and a future" (Jeremiah 29:11). He knows your heart, and He will give you your desires, so "seek first His kingdom and His righteousness, and all these things will be given to you as well" (Matthew 6:33).

BREATHE: Words to Impact Your Prayers

Acknowledge and Admit:

Lord, You are the One who knows the future and my potential in it.

I don't even know my own heart and mind sometimes.

Appreciate and Ask:

Thank You for placing in my heart desires that come from You.

*I ask You to lead me, as you bring about
Your plans and purposes for my life.*

LAP 16

YOU ARE ENOUGH

FOCUS: Words to Prepare Your Mind

"Whatever you have today is enough. It might not look like it to you, but put into Jesus' hands, it is more than enough."

- Sheila Walsh, Imagine Devotional Journal

"You made all the delicate, inner parts of my body and knit me together in my mother's womb. Thank You for making me so wonderfully complex! Your workmanship is marvelous—how well I know it"

(Psalm 139:13-14 NLT).

PUSH: Words to Influence Your Spirit

Do you ever feel 'less than' and wonder if you have what it takes to accomplish anything? Do you believe that your value lies in your accomplishments?

When we define ourselves by the things we do—I guarantee you—we will always feel that it is never enough. We will feel compelled to do more, and then more, and then more. It is impossible to measure up to that standard on a long-term basis *and* have peace of mind. We continually 'do, do, do,' and then we wonder why we aren't happy. Unfortunately, it seems that this is the way a vast number of people view life. And, from time to time, I am guilty of it too. So if you find yourself in a place like this today, you are not alone.

It is important for us to know this: When we are God's children, we are 'enough' to live the life that He has planned for us to live. Now, I know that holding on to this can be tough because, when we are quiet and still, we can be deeply impacted by the words God says about us and to us. But when our everyday life gets busy and hectic, we tend to forget what He said. So make a point to remember this; the beauty of life is that God never intended for us to live in performance mode, thinking that, if we do this or that, God will love us more. That thought is simply not the truth. God wants to know that our heart belongs to Him. I am telling you now; Jesus Christ has already *done* the hard part. He has accomplished the impossible for us! Jesus died on the cross so we could be forgiven and brought back into a relationship with God, and He was raised to life so that we, too, can have life eternally through Him. There is nothing we can think, say or do to make God love us any more than He already does. He loves us completely. He created us in His perfect image. He knew what we were going to be like from our earliest moments. "You created my inmost being; you knit me together in my mother's womb" (Psalm 139:13). So I am sure that it hurts the heart of God when we beat ourselves up and allow the lies of Satan to defeat us. Jesus told us that Satan "comes only to steal and kill and destroy" (John 10:1). He wants to eliminate us in any and every way possible. I am sure Satan loves it when we feel like we're 'less than,' when we feel like we have to be this way or that for someone to acknowledge that we are enough. I say this because God works to remind me of this on a regular basis. Like I said, I have a tendency to 'do, do, do,' and like so many others it leaves me feeling empty inside. At times like that, I feel as though I can't even measure up to myself, let alone anyone else, and especially God. However, Jesus continually tells me, "No! You *are* enough! Trust that 'I have come that [you] may have life, and have it to the full' (John 10:10). I have shown you this by dying for your sins and rising from the dead."

So I encourage you today, and myself as well; let yourself off the hook. Learn about all God has created you to be, and focus on *being* rather than *doing*. You are enough. You don't have to prove anything to anyone. After all, what God thinks is all that matters. He loves you and accepts you right where you are. Receive His love and be open to the changes He wants to bring about. Hopefully, you know that growth needs to take place if you still struggle between an effort-driven "do" mentality and an identity-based "be" mentality. Of course, we all struggle with this from time to time. But rest assured; God still loves you. That is why He won't let you get away with not learning what He wants to teach you before He moves you on to the next phase in your life. Take one day at a time, and trust that He knows what is best for you.

BREATHE: Words to Impact Your Prayers

Acknowledge and Admit:

Lord, You are the God who loves and restores me.

I struggle with whether or not I am adequate enough to live the life You want for me.

Appreciate and Ask:

*Thank You for loving me where I am,
and loving me too much to leave me there.*

I ask You to help me know that, with Your Holy Spirit, I am enough.

LAP 17

NOTHING IS IMPOSSIBLE WITH GOD

FOCUS: Words to Prepare Your Mind

"When we put our faith and trust in God, we've done the one thing that a human can do to accomplish superhuman things. We have reached past human strength and knowledge. We've touched infinite strength and infinite knowledge."

**- Henry Cloud, God Will Make a Way:
What to Do When You Don't Know What to Do**

"Jesus looked at them and said, 'With man this is impossible, but with God all things are possible'"
(Matthew 19:26).

PUSH: Words to Influence Your Spirit

Do you ever ask, "Where are You, God? Do You even see the impossible situation I am in?"

We pray and pray, and it just doesn't feel as though God is answering. I can tell you today that God does hear our prayers and He is working behind the scenes for us even when we don't *feel* that He is.

There was a time when I owned my own business. I felt as though I should sell it—I didn't want to close it down—and yet, there were no buyers on the horizon. One day, I heard about someone who was in the market to buy a business like mine. So we got together and discussed it, but things just didn't work out. And, like I always do, I kept moving forward.

I thought about expanding my business. However, I began to sense God speaking to me. Have you ever been thinking about pursuing a second option, but the first option—the one that didn't work out—keeps coming back to you? This is one of the ways I know that God is trying to talk to me. It is like He keeps bringing it back to my mind until I get it.

Nothing was working out with the expansion of the business. I needed clarity on what to do, so I decided to go on a fast with God. That same day—out of a clear blue sky—the woman who months earlier had been looking for a business like mine called me. She said, "God told me that I need to buy your business." My jaw hit the floor! Talk about making the impossible possible!

God knew my heart's desire, and I kept my heart open to what He had for me. I was obedient to Him by waiting for Him to open and close the doors. I decided to fast in the first place so I could have a clear picture of the direction God wanted me to go. I truly believe that when we are patient and wait for God to act, He will make His direction clear to us. But it has to be in His timing; not our own.

So I encourage you today that, whatever prayer you might be waiting on God to answer, just be still and know that God is working behind the scenes. His timing will be the perfect timing for you. He can make possible what seems impossible.

BREATHE: Words to Impact Your Prayers

Acknowledge and Admit:

Lord, You are the God of both the possible and the impossible.

I need to learn patience as I wait for You to answer my prayers and give me direction.

Appreciate and Ask:

Thank You for working behind the scenes on my behalf.

I ask You to help me be still as You make impossible things possible in my life.

LAP 18

RECEIVE HIS PEACE

FOCUS: Words to Prepare Your Mind

"When you accept rather than fight your circumstances, even though you don't understand them, you open your heart's gate to God's love, peace, joy, and contentment."

- Amy Carmichael, Hugs: Daily Inspirations for Women

"Peace I leave with you; My peace I give you. I do not give to you as the world gives. Do not let your hearts be troubled and do not be afraid"

(John 14:27).

PUSH: Words to Influence Your Spirit

Are you struggling to find true peace in an area of your life?

I believe that peace is one of the deepest needs people have, and one of the hardest things to maintain in our everyday lives. There are so many things that get in the way of experiencing God's peace. And it is Satan who wants to rob our peace on a continual basis.

In Sarah Young's *Jesus Calling* devotional, she offers really good insight on having peace in our lives. "When I start to worry, or fear I just start thanking Jesus for His peace presence regardless of my feelings, just start whispering His name in a sweet loving tenderness and God's peace will work through your entire being...Peace lives continually in your spirit you just have not to allow it to be taken away."

Looking back through the years, I have found that it is when I seem to lose God's peace and have allowed the influence of the world get in my way that I know it is time for me to go on a fast with God. Once I decide to fast, the presence of God just comes over me. That's when I find the peace and rest

I have been longing for. That's when I have a clear mind to hear what God wants to tell me and an open heart to anything that He has for me. And this is what God strongly desires for each of us.

Sarah Young also talks about how His peace is a continual gift to us and the best way to receive this gift is to sit quietly in His presence trusting Him in every area of our life. Quietness and trust accomplish far more than we can imagine. When we live close to Him, it is a sure defense against evil.

So I encourage you today to make it your goal to continually live in peace. To do that you must live in the full presence of God, and when you are, you will find the peace that you want.

BREATHE: Words to Impact Your Prayers

Acknowledge and Admit:

Lord, You are the Prince of Peace.

I am sometimes swayed by things around me, which steal away my peace.

Appreciate and Ask:

Thank You for clearing my mind and opening my heart when I am focused on You.

I ask You to remind me on a daily basis that I can experience Your peace.

LAP 19

RECEIVE HIS STRENGTH

FOCUS: Words to Prepare Your Mind

"God grant me the serenity to accept the things I cannot change, courage to change the things I can, and wisdom to know the difference."

- Reinhold Niebuhr, Serenity Prayer

"I can do everything through Christ, who gives me strength"

(Philippians 4:13 NLT).

PUSH: Words to Influence Your Spirit

Did you ever have one of those days when you needed God to give you a little extra *oomph* just to get you through it all?

Keep asking God for strength. If you're not already asking, start now. God wants us to come to Him for the things we need. He will give us the strength we need when we need it because He is our strength.

God constantly reminds me that I don't have to do things alone, that He is there for me as my leader and guide. He says, "Follow me. Let go of your burdens, and let me carry you through." When you do, you will find rest and peace because God is all-powerful. When we put our trust in Him and rely on Him, we will find the strength we need. There may be times when we feel like giving up, but God gives us a constant reminder; "He said to me [the Apostle Paul], 'My grace is sufficient for you, for my power is made perfect in weakness.' Therefore I will boast all the more gladly about my weaknesses, so that Christ's power may rest on me" (2 Corinthians 12:9).

So I encourage you today to trust God for His grace and believe it today, and you will get through anything. Let go, and let God be your strength. And when you feel like giving up, don't, because God will never give up on you.

BREATHE: Words to Impact Your Prayers

Acknowledge and Admit:

Lord, You are strong.

I am weak.

Appreciate and Ask:

Thank You for Your love and graciousness, which are enough for me.

I ask You to make Your strength known through my weakness.

LAP 20

RECEIVE HIS PROVISION

FOCUS: Words to Prepare Your Mind

"God is there for us in bigger ways than we could ever think or ask."

- Nicole Johnson, Imagine Devotional Journal

"My God will meet all your needs according to the riches of his glory in Christ Jesus"

(Philippians 4:19).

PUSH: Words to Influence Your Spirit

Do you believe that God has your back and that He wants to provide for your every need?

God is watching out for us, protecting us, and providing for us because He wants the best for us. And do you know why? It's because He loves us so much. There is nothing we can say or do that will ever change the way He feels about us.

God knows all of our needs, and there is nothing that He cannot do to meet our needs. When we wish that God would just remove all of our troubles from life, we have to remember verses like this; "He rescued me from my powerful enemy, from my foes, who were too strong for me. They confronted me in the day of my disaster, but the Lord was my support" (Psalm 18:17–18). God "rescues us from," and He "supports us through" our troubles. Either way, His presence is best for us no matter what. When we feel like we are drowning in our troubles, we cannot be afraid to ask for God's help, to hold us steady and protect us. With God, we are never helpless.

Many people wrongly think that relying on God is a crutch for weak people who cannot make it on their own. Let this be settled in your heart; that idea is the exact opposite of the truth. The Bible talks about the fact that "as for God, His way is perfect: the Lord's word is flawless; He shields all who take refuge in Him" (Psalm 18:30). God is the shield that protects us when we are too weak to face trials by ourselves. But, the one thing that He doesn't want is for us to remain weak. He wants to strengthen us, protect us, and guide us, so that, while we are out here in this fallen, evil world, we can stand strong and fight for Him. We cannot let our daily struggles hold us back from being all that God created us to be. He will, and He does provide for us. All we have to do is ask Him.

The Bible says, "It is God who arms me with strength and keeps my way secure. He makes my feet like the feet of a deer; he causes me to stand on the heights. He trains my hands for battle; my arms can bend a bow of bronze" (Psalm 18:32–34). He doesn't promise to eliminate our challenges but to give us the strength to meet every one of them head on. After all, if there were no mountains to climb, rough roads to walk, no battles to fight, how would we grow? God promises to never leave us alone on those mountains, down those roads, or in those battles. He stands beside us, teaches us, and strengthens us to face our challenges.

While I was on one of my fasts with God, I gained an even clearer understanding of how He takes care of me personally and provides for my needs. My accountant called about one of the businesses I owned at that time. He let me know that my previous accountant had not filed a certain form and the oversight was going to cost me thousands of dollars. . . and that the deadline to pay was "real soon." As you can imagine, a moment of panic (maybe two) came over me. However, I decided to not let Satan get the best of my emotions, and I stepped out in faith, believing that God would provide for my need. Faithfully, God did exactly that, and I paid off the money I owed by the due date I had been given.

Soon after this, I realized that a tax deadline was coming up. And, I was in the middle of planning and preparing for my wedding.

My accountant called me. (By the way, I was on a fast with God during this time, too.) He said, "I cannot believe this, but not only do you *not* have to pay this year, but you are being refunded *thousands* of dollars. And I am not sure I can explain to you how it happened."

I smiled as tears welled up in my eyes, "God knew just what I needed for my wedding."

God knows and cares about the details of our lives—like an exact amount of money needed for a wedding—and He provides for His children because He is faithful. No, He did not say everything was going to be easy. God saw the bigger picture of my life, and He knew I would grow, personally and professionally, in those times.

What I know now is that, no matter what I go through, God is always there and He provides for me at just the right time. So I encourage you today that, when you think all hope is gone, think again, because God has ways of providing even when we least expect it.

BREATHE: Words to Impact Your Prayers

Acknowledge and Admit:

Lord, You are a limitless God, and there is nothing You cannot do.

I often panic when the unexpected happens.

Appreciate and Ask:

*Thank You for loving me and taking care of me
by providing for my needs.*

*I ask You to help me trust You and believe that You love me
and will continue to care for my needs.*

LAP 21

RECEIVE HIS BLESSING

FOCUS: Words to Prepare Your Mind

"Be a blessing to others, and you will be blessed."
- Joyce Meyer, The Life in the Word Devotional

"The Lord bless you and keep you; the Lord make His face shine on you and be gracious to you; the Lord turn His face toward you and give you peace"
(Numbers 6:24-26).

PUSH: Words to Influence Your Spirit

Did you know that God wants to bless us abundantly, but sometimes we don't see His blessings in our life simply because we don't ask for them?

I learned this when I read a book called *The Prayer of Jabez* by Bruce Wilkinson. If you haven't read this amazing book, or haven't read it lately, I highly recommend that you do. It was life-changing for me in the sense that it encouraged me to start asking God for His blessings. I realized that asking for things God wants to do for us anyway is okay. It is not a selfish act like many people feel. The book also made it clear to me that God wants to bless us all the time.

This premise of that book is based on a simple prayer that is found tucked away in the middle of nine chapters filled with hundreds and hundreds of names. "'Oh, that you would bless me and enlarge my territory! Let your hand be with me, and keep me from harm so that I will be free from pain.' And God granted his request" (1 Chronicles 4:10). I believe that every time

I pray that prayer and ask God for those kinds of blessings, He has blessed me in more ways than I could ever imagine.

Since I started praying that prayer, God brought my amazing husband, Bryan, into my life. He has blessed us with two healthy, beautiful children. He has surrounded me with people who have made, and continue to make, a big difference in my life. He has increased my businesses—quite honestly, the list goes on and on. But, I believe that one of the most important things that God has done through *The Prayer of Jabez*, as well as my own prayer life, is that He has opened my eyes to really *see* all of the blessings He has given.

So I encourage you today to keep your eyes open to all the blessings God has for you and wants to bring into your life. It can often be easier for us to focus on the things we are not getting or on the negative things happening in our lives. But know this, God is for you and not against you. He wants to give you all of the blessings that He has for you, but, the Bible says, "You do not have because you do not ask God. When you ask, you do not receive, because you ask with wrong motives" (James 4:2–3). So *ask*, with the right heart, because Jesus promised, "Ask and it will be given to you; seek and you will find; knock and the door will be opened to you" (Matthew 7:7). When you start seeing the blessings God has for you because you asked, whether big or small, you will thank Him with a truly grateful heart. After all, when we have a thankful heart, God can continue to bless us. And remember; a blessing can be something you don't even recognize as a blessing at the time. Because God knows the future, He knows just what you need and right when you need it.

BREATHE: Words to Impact Your Prayers

Acknowledge and Admit:

Lord, You are the God who blesses me.

I am limited in seeing how much You really do bless me.

Appreciate and Ask:

Thank You for the blessings I see clearly and the ones I want to recognize more in my life.

I ask You to bless me and help me keep my focus on You, not just the wonderful things You give.

LAP 22

BE THANKFUL

FOCUS: Words to Prepare Your Mind

"A sense of gratitude will help open our eyes to the things God has done in the past and the things He will do in the future."

- Emilie Barnes, Hugs: Daily Inspirations for Women

"Always [give] thanks to God the Father for everything, in the name of our Lord Jesus Christ"

(Ephesians 5:20).

PUSH: Words to Influence Your Spirit

Do you believe that God is good, that He has your best interest in mind, and that He wants you to be successful in everything He has for you? Did you know that having a mindset like this will always lead to a thankful heart?

In everything we do, in all circumstances, we are to thank God. He sees the bigger picture, and He is not going to allow something good nor bad to happen without making sure that the result will give Him all the praise and glory.

I am going to share one of my stories with you, but I am not going to focus on details. I want you to see the dynamics of what I went through instead. I worked on a deal for my job for an entire year. There were times during that year when I didn't know what else I could do. I felt as though I had no control. However, I kept sensing that in His still, small voice, God was saying, "Trust Me. It is all going to work out. Thank Me. Thank Me while you wait." That's easier said than done, right? I worked and prayed and waited and thanked God. My flesh would worry consistently, but my heart would always be at peace. I worked. I went on fasts with God, to seek Him for some clearer answers. I waited. And I thanked Him. You know the saying "There's a light is at the end of the tunnel"? When we are going through times like this, we wonder about that light. We wonder if things are ever going to "end well." All along the way, I had my doubts about the situation, but God was always there. When I allowed myself to worry, it exposed my lack of trust, but I thanked God in spite of my feelings. I knew that worry is not from Him; it is not where He wants us to live.

Finally, everything came together. And I thanked God.

I can look back on the situation now and see that God was waiting for the right timing. But in the meantime, it felt as though He was testing me to see how much I was going to trust Him. Was I going to trust Him to accomplish His will or was I going to give up and demand that my own way happens? Even though it may have felt like that, I actually saw something different at work; God strengthened me and developed in me a heart of thankfulness. In the end, God knew what I needed and when I needed it. And I was better off because of the process. One of the most awesome things about going through times like this is seeing everything work out for God's glory. His timing is everything. He isn't going to allow something to happen or come to an end until we have learned all He wants us to learn through that time of waiting.

So I encourage you today to give Him thanks in everything you do. I promise; He will never let you down.

BREATHE: Words to Impact Your Prayers

Acknowledge and Admit:

Lord, You are worthy of my gratitude and praise.

I forget that Your Word, the Bible, tells me to "give thanks in all circumstances."

Appreciate and Ask:

Thank You, Lord. Just thank You.

I ask You to fill my heart with trust and peace; thankfulness and praise.

LAP 23

LOVE RADICALLY

FOCUS: Words to Prepare Your Mind

"When we know that we are loved by God, loved beyond measure, we can dive in and take a chance."

- Sheila Walsh, Imagine Devotional Journal

"God so loved the world that He gave His one and only Son, that whoever believes in Him shall not perish but have eternal life"

(John 3:16).

PUSH: Words to Influence Your Spirit

Would you consider your love for Jesus to be 'radical love'?

Whether you feel that your love for Jesus is radical or not, know this: Jesus is radically in love with you.

Let me tell you what radical love means. It is having an all-consuming, passionate love for God—the kind of love God has for you. Do you want this radical kind of love in your life? If you do, let me tell you how to get it.

First and foremost, if you don't have it, you have to confess that fact. Secondly, cry out to God for it in your life. And lastly, don't give up until you get it!

The greatest demonstration of God's radical love for us is the cross of Jesus Christ. God did the most amazing thing—something no mere human could ever bear to do. The day Jesus died on the cross, He took all of our sins away. The pain He went through for you and me was unimaginable. But, incredibly, He loved us so much that He did it. And I thank God every day for His death on the cross so that I could have eternal life. It is amazing to think about.

So I encourage you today; if you want to live a radical life, you need to have a radical love for Jesus. Radical love results in a radical life. I don't know about you, but I want the radical life that God has planned for me. It is extravagant and vastly different from any form of legalistic religion. When you have radical love—when you *love* radically, you also experience God's peace, contentment, and true and lasting joy. More than this, you will experience freedom. Freedom is less a physical thing, and more a heart thing. Radical lives always bring the radical love of God to a needy world, and we need it more than ever now. Wouldn't you agree? Always remember; when you have radical love, it changes more than one life.

BREATHE: Words to Impact Your Prayers

Acknowledge and Admit:

Lord, You are the greatest example of radical love.

My love tends to be exclusive to those I deem lovable.

Appreciate and Ask:

Thank You for demonstrating Your love through the cross.

I ask You to help me know Your love better and share it with anyone and everyone.

LAP 24

DEVELOP YOUR OBEDIENCE

FOCUS: Words to Prepare Your Mind

"We feel a calling inside that's bigger than ourselves. It's an invisible force on the horizon, pulling us toward it. What is that? It's God."

- **Luci Swindoll, Imagine Devotional Journal**

*"In their hearts humans plan their course,
but the Lord establishes their steps"*

(Proverbs 16:9).

PUSH: Words to Influence Your Spirit

Are you listening to hear God's voice? Are you hearing what He is saying? Most importantly, are you being obedient in what you hear?

I'm not sure about you, but personally, I struggle a lot with whose voice it is that I am hearing. Is it God's voice or am I just telling myself what I want to hear? Is that Satan deceiving me? Is God testing me in certain areas of my life to see how in tune I am with Him? More than this, if it is God, am I willing to listen and go above and beyond and do what God is telling me to do?

I'll be honest, it's sometimes difficult for me to differentiate God's voice from mine. Someone once gave me some advice for when we wonder whether we are hearing from God or not. If what we're hearing is morally okay, if it's not dangerous or will harm yourself or someone else, then we should try to move in that direction. Whether we know for sure if it is from God or not, I truly believe God will steer us in the direction we should go, and that He will open and close the doors along the way. I will also say that, based on years of experience with prayer and fasting, I have come to a personal conclusion. When something keeps coming back to my mind—whatever the circumstance may be—and I experience peace about it, then I can be confident that it is God who is talking to me. And we can never go wrong by being obedient to what God is telling us to do.

I recently received some of the biggest blessings from God because I felt like He was speaking to me. I went ahead and moved forward in what He asked me to do. I was stepping out in faith, believing that God would lead me down the right path. I was standing on the promise of Jesus; "Seek first his kingdom and his righteousness, and all these things [food, water, and clothing] will be given to you as well" (Matthew 6:33).

One of the blessings I received from my obedience involved hosting a ministry academy student in our home. God had placed in my husband's heart and mine a desire to be a host family for a student at our church. However, when I called, the church said they were already filled up and didn't need any more host families. A couple of weeks went by, and it kept coming back up to my mind to call again. Finally, I did, and a young woman had just signed up that day and was in need of a host family. I thought, "Wow, was that God or what?" It was a huge faith-builder which allowed me to know that we had heard from God! The young woman that came and lived with us has been the biggest blessing to our family. She is such a great role model for our children. She loves Jesus with all of her heart. And since that time, she has come back during summers and vacation times to help take care of our children. I truly believe that when we are obedient to God, He just makes things in our life flow. By being obedient and stepping out in faith, I received an unexpected blessing. God knows what is best for us, and He honors our obedience when we take the time just to sit and listen to what He is asking of us.

Now, I have also been on the other end, where I knew God was asking me to do something, but I avoided saying yes. I pushed it off and, wanting to ignore and forget what He said, I kept living my life. Of course, I never forgot what He said. He has His ways of not letting us forget things sometimes. For a year, I continued to avoid what God told me to do, and I ended up being miserable. I felt like my faith was constantly being tested. Things were not going as well as they had been in years past. I had a lot of anxiety, discouragement, the list goes on and on. I can say now that I won't ever recommend saying *no* to God.

However, looking back, I now realize that God gives us freedom of choice. We might think the decisions we make are good for us, but God sees the end result. We can pray for something so much, and God can allow us to have whatever it is that we are praying for. When God allows me to have my will and not necessarily His, am I happy? No! Am I at peace? No! I thought I was what I wanted, and God allowed it. But as I continued to move forward in it, I felt like God was saying, "Okay, are you tired yet? Are you ready to listen to Me now?" Sometimes, we might just have to go through things just to realize it is not all that we thought it was going to be. I will say I finally got that lesson, and once I did, peace came over me and blessings started to pour into my life.

So I encourage you today that, when God speaks to you, really listen and obey. The blessings and the fulfillment of joy that He gives you when you are obedient to His Word are amazing. It is not only the joy and blessings that come from being obedient but also the eternal blessings you will receive in heaven, which are far greater than anything you will receive on earth.

BREATHE: Words to Impact Your Prayers

Acknowledge and Admit:

Lord, You are the God who speaks to me.

I often struggle with whether I can hear Your voice, or if it is really You speaking to me.

Appreciate and Ask:

Thank You for loving me enough to continue speaking even when I don't understand.

I ask You to help me hear You, understand what You are saying, and to embrace it fully.

LAP 25

DEVELOP YOUR FAITH

FOCUS: Words to Prepare Your Mind

"Through faith, we have the opportunity to watch the God of the universe do the impossible in our lives."

- Imagine, Imagine Devotional Journal

"Though you have not seen Him, you love Him; and even though you do not see Him now, you believe in Him and are filled with an inexpressible and glorious joy, for you are receiving the end result of your faith, the salvation of your souls"

(1 Peter 1:8-9).

PUSH: Words to Influence Your Spirit

Do you believe that "God is who He says He is, and He will do what He says He will do?"

Our pastor defines 'faith' in this way and reminds us of this truth in many of his sermons.

Read that first line over and over again until you can accept it, believe it, and use it as a part of your daily life. In the Bible, the wording may be different, but I think the meaning is the same. "Faith is confidence in what we hope for and assurance about what we do not see" (Hebrews 11:1).

For me—although it is *sometimes* easy to express faith in my life—I often find it one of the hardest things for me to do. Since faith is about things that are unseen, I struggle with it at times. I like seeing things ahead. I would rather know God's plan in full, so I can prepare for what is coming. Can you relate to this? I have quickly realized that this is not how God works. And I continue to realize this day after day.

You see, God's timing is in God's time. And what I have learned and continue to see is that God's timing is also at the right time. At this point in my life, I just wouldn't want it any other way. As we continue to trust God and allow Him to work in our lives—let go of our own need to control—He will begin to work out His plan and desires for us. He will then be able to work through us and be able to do great things in us when we allow Him to.

God continues to bless my life. I look at all of the things that have happened in my life that have been faith-builders for me. I would like to share the dynamics rather than the details of a couple of them with you. I think you'll get the idea.

I had been praying and fasting with God on a weekly basis for a few months. One day, I prayed and asked God to please allow something great to happen with one of my jobs. What I prayed, though, was very specific. The day after praying that prayer, God answered it exactly the way I had asked for it to happen.

Another time, I was praying about one of my relationships, and God specifically told me to wait to do anything until a certain date. So I continued to simply pray and fast until that date came. And, on the date that He had told me to wait for, God gave me the answer.

I tell you these stories from my life to let you know that experiences in our lives like these are faith-builders. When we know that God is speaking to us, all we have to do is listen to His voice, be still, and wait for Him to act on our behalf. This is what I did in those examples, and I believe that God honored my obedience in each case. When God continues to show us His faithfulness, it strengthens and reconfirms our faith. We become confident that God will do what He says He will do. Sometimes, it's just a matter of us being patient. It's a matter of trusting, and believing, and waiting for God to act. When we rely on God in this way, our faith continues to grow more and more. I ask you; what are the faith-builders from God that you have seen in your life? Have you even allowed Him to build your faith?

So I encourage you today; God is faithful even when we are not. He promised; "You will call on Me and come and pray to Me, and I will listen to you. You will seek Me and find Me when you seek Me with all your heart" (Jeremiah 29:12–13). I know from my own experience that God will answer your prayers. Now, it might not be exactly how you want the prayer to be answered, but it will be the way God wants to answer it. And we should only want what God wants for us. He foresees the future and wants the absolute best. So, some of those answered (or unanswered) prayers just could be the blessing you have been waiting for—the one God wants to bring into your life. When you pray continually about a concern, don't be surprised about how God answers. God's ways of answering our prayers are often far from what we expect. When you sincerely pray, God will sometimes answer at times, and in ways you don't expect.

BREATHE: Words to Impact Your Prayers

Acknowledge and Admit:

*Lord, You are who You say You are and
will do what You say You will do.*

I need to see your faithfulness, so my faith will grow.

Appreciate and Ask:

Thank You for the faith-builders You have brought about in my life.

*I ask You to give me more and more opportunities
to see You at work in my life.*

LAP 26

DEVELOP GENEROSITY, PT. 1 (THE WHOLE HEART)

FOCUS: Words to Prepare Your Mind

"Offering yourself to God is what worship is all about."

- Rick Warren, The Purpose Driven Life

"A poor widow came and put in two very small copper coins, worth only a few cents. Calling His disciples to Him, Jesus said, 'Truly I tell you, this poor widow has put more into the treasury than all the others. They all gave out of their wealth; but she, out of her poverty, put in everything–all she had to live on'"

(Mark 12:42-44).

PUSH: Words to Influence Your Spirit

Have you ever noticed that when you give something—whether a smile, a present, or yourself and your time—you seem to feel almost as good as the person receiving your gift?

I truly believe that when you give something, you receive a blessing back in return. It might not be the same thing or things that you receive back. It could be as little as the joy that you feel inside for being able to bless someone else.

I know I can struggle in this area. Sometimes, I feel that, if I were to lose my income or give away my money, then I wouldn't have it when I needed it. I would be too broke to get the things "I want." However, I have found that this way of thinking is just my insecure selfishness talking to me. It's the kind of thinking Satan wants me to be paralyzed by. However, when I am in the presence of God and everything is in His hands, I have the peace and freedom which God desires for me to have. He continually reminds me that none of these things are mine, and to see them as blessings He has provided for my family and me. God has given me a family that is healthy. He has provided a roof over our heads and enough food for us to eat (I can go on and on and on). What more do I need?

The world says that we need a newer car or a bigger house or a better this or that to make us happy. It tells us that more and more money equals more and more success. I want to tell you that God couldn't care less about the world's standards for happiness and success. He is not looking at the size of our bank account but the size of our heart. He is watching *how* we use our money—whether we have plenty to spare or barely enough to scrape by. He loves us all the same, and He wants to see us use money wisely and for the sake of His kingdom.

One holiday season, my extended family didn't want to do as much, in terms of Christmas gifts, as we usually do for one another. Instead, we wanted to provide a really special blessing to other families outside of our own. So we were praying about who it was God wanted us to give to. A friend of mine told me about an organization called "Through Our Children's Lives." When I called them, I kept getting a busy signal. But I kept hearing God tell me to keep trying to call. I placed call after call and, finally, was able to get through. They were actually closed that day, but there was a worker who happened to be there. She went ahead and answered the phone. When I told her we were looking to bless one or more families through their organization, she told me that three families had been dropped. (This all happened just two days before Christmas.) Wow! Does God work in miraculous ways or what? My heart instantly filled up, and I knew that those three families were the families we were to bless this season. And, as it turned out, there just happened to be three of my extended family members who hadn't found a family to adopt yet. I remember the feeling that day as we gave to those families. It was the biggest blessing to be able to give and help others. Just knowing those little kids were going to have a good Christmas was the highlight of our holiday season. Those families will never know who blessed them at Christmas, but God knows because He is the One who made that blessing happen.

So I encourage you today that, if God is laying on your heart to give to someone or some cause—whether it is money, time, a special word of encouragement—don't wait. Just do it! It may not only bless their lives but yours as well.

BREATHE: Words to Impact Your Prayers

Acknowledge and Admit:

Lord, You are the most generous example of someone who gives and blesses.

I sometimes forget about needs that exist beyond my own family.

Appreciate and Ask:

Thank You for blessing me to be a blessing to others.

I ask You to lead and direct my generosity according to Your will.

LAP 27

DEVELOP GENEROSITY, PT. 2 (THE TENTH PART)

FOCUS: Words to Prepare Your Mind

"If you are measuring out your offering to God, you have never truly seen His true worth."

- Wick Neese, (Quoted from a sermon)

"Jesus sat down opposite the place where the offerings were put and watched the crowd putting their money into the temple treasury. Many rich people threw in large amounts"

(Mark 12:41).

PUSH: Words to Influence Your Spirit

Did you know that everything belongs to God, that every created thing belongs to its Creator?

All of our money, our possessions, even our body—*everything*—belongs to God. "The earth is the Lord's, and everything in it, the world, and all who live in it" (Psalm 24:1). We act as though the things which are on loan to us are really "our things," that we own them, not just manage them. So most of us have a difficult time allowing ourselves to trust God completely with things, especially money.

One of the ways God wants us to use our money is by tithing to the church. He asks that we give a tithe (a tenth) of all of our earnings, right off the top. The Bible shows us this where it says, "As soon as the order went out, the

Israelites generously gave the firstfruits of their grain, new wine, olive oil and honey and all that the fields produced. They brought a great amount, a tithe of everything" (2 Chronicles 31:5). When we are obedient with our money and give our tithe, God blesses and honors that act.

I am a person who tithes. I always give God at least ten percent of my earnings, sometimes more. I find that when I do, God blesses me and provides for all of my needs. It is not that He always blesses me back with more money, but I can say that I have never gone without and He has provided more than I even deserve.

I had been on a fast with God, off and on, for a couple of weeks. During that time, I heard God say to me, "Give this money to a certain person, and I want it to be done anonymously." So I did, and I didn't think twice about it. Then, I felt God laid it on my heart to give more—a full ten percent to the church. "But, I just gave 'my tithe' to someone else." I figured that my tithe is when I give something extra to someone in need. However, the Bible talks about giving the first ten percent to the church. I didn't completely understand that, not until this situation where God asked me to do go above and beyond ten percent. What I realized was that He was not asking me to do more—just the ten percent that is required of me. The extra money I gave was just something God asked me to do, so I was doing it out of obedience. When God asks me to do something, I don't want to ignore Him. I want to be obedient. God honors obedience, as it says in the Bible; "From everyone who has been given much, much will be demanded; and from the one who has been entrusted with much, much more will be asked" (Luke 12:48). But I will admit that, during that time, the fleshly part of me wanted to be selfish and hold on to that money. However, I knew in my heart that I had learned my lesson before—not to ignore God when He is speaking to me. I always seem to know when God is talking to me. Through all of this, I heard God tell me that I would not be sorry and He promised He would provide. This just shows how God is so faithful.

The following week, two business deals I had been praying would go through did exactly that. And an additional deal that I wasn't even expecting also went through. Both what I gave and what I made from those deals was greater than I expected. He rewards those who are obedient and faithful to Him.

So I encourage you today to not hold back. Give your ten percent to God because that is just being obedient to what He asks of us. You will be amazed at how God's blessings pour out upon your life when you are obedient with the tithe. I always remember something my mom used to say; "You can never out give God." I know God's faithfulness enough to know that God will never let you down. It's all God's money anyway. If you're not tithing, choose to be obedient and tithe. Even if you only have ten dollars to your name, giving that one dollar can change your life forever.

BREATHE: Words to Impact Your Prayers

Acknowledge and Admit:

Lord, You are the Creator of everything, and it all belongs to You.

I tend to be possessive of things I am only managing for You.

Appreciate and Ask:

Thank You for opportunities to put You first through my tithe.

I ask You to help me be faithful with everything You put into my hands.

LAP 28

DEVELOP GRATITUDE

FOCUS: Words to Prepare Your Mind

"Life, for the most part, is what we make it. We have been given a responsibility to live it fully, joyfully, completely, and richly, in whatever span of time God grants us on this earth."

- Luci Swindoll, A Grand New Day

"Rejoice always, pray continually, give thanks in all circumstances; for this is God's will for you in Christ Jesus"

(1 Thessalonians 5:16-18).

PUSH: Words to Influence Your Spirit

Would you describe yourself, generally, as a thankful person or as someone who doesn't often feel gratitude?

Ungratefulness is when you are always focused on what you do not have rather than being grateful for what you do have. I don't know if this is an area you struggle with, but I know that my selfish flesh struggles with this at times. If you do as well, you are not alone.

God wants us to have a spirit of thankfulness all the time—no matter what our circumstances might be. The Bible tells us to "give thanks in all circumstances; for this is God's will for you in Christ Jesus" (1 Thessalonians 5:18). That means that even when things don't seem to go as planned. We can be thankful in difficult times because God sees the bigger picture. He knows what is right around the corner for us. And no matter what, He wants to teach us something through those times that don't seem easy. Look for the things that God is trying to teach you in your everyday life, whether good or bad. It is always easier to see the negative in things rather than the positive. So today, seek God and ask Him to open your eyes to find the things that you are grateful for. Start coming to Him in prayer with a spirit of thankfulness instead of focusing on the things you do not have or the needs that aren't being met. When you change your focus to the things that God is doing in your life, you will find that it will change your outlook on the way you see everything else. God knows the outcome. Until He allows us to see what He wants us to see, He might just keep us waiting for the answer we have been longing to have.

Just recently, I was on a fast with God. (Before I share this story with you, let me say that God might not give you the answer you are looking for during your fast, but I believe that, in due time, He will give you an answer, whether it is the one you're looking for or not. Through my past experiences, I believe that this is where faith comes in—truly believing what you cannot see yet. Believe God has your best interest at heart, and that He will never let you down.) During this particular fast, I had such a spirit of thankfulness. God has opened and closed doors for my husband and me regarding the direction we are headed, and at this point, we have options. To be in this place is refreshing. We don't know whether any of our options will come about, but God does. We only know—in light of things we have been praying about—that we are on the right path, going in the right direction.

Two years earlier, God told us that I was to let one of my careers go. He said that we would see my husband's business flourish, and to not worry because He would provide for all our financial needs. The peace I experienced was so much greater than I could ever imagine. I will say that God has never failed me, and I know He won't fail you either. Here is one thing I know; as we continue along on the journey God has prepared for us, God asks us to keep pressing on. God never said it would be easy, but He did tell us to "take delight in the Lord, and he will give you the desires of your heart" (Psalm 37:4).

So I encourage you today that, no matter where you are, you can give God thanks in every situation. Know that you are His child. And just like we want the best for our children, He wants the very best for you.

BREATHE: Words to Impact Your Prayers

Acknowledge and Admit:

Lord, You are the reason I can be grateful in every circumstance I face.

I let my judgment of whether a situation is good or bad govern my gratitude.

Appreciate and Ask:

Thank You for loving me, even though I cannot thank You enough.

I ask You to help me be more thankful, not just to You but to others as well.

LAP 29

BE PATIENT

FOCUS: Words to Prepare Your Mind

*"Patience is not simply the ability to wait;
it's how we behave while we're waiting."*

**- Joyce Meyer, Battlefield of the Mind:
Winning the Battle in Your Mind**

*"Those who hope in the Lord will renew their strength.
They will soar on wings like eagles; they will run and not grow weary,
they will walk and not be faint"*

(Isaiah 40:31).

PUSH: Words to Influence Your Spirit

Do you feel like you spend most of your time waiting on God to answer your prayers and act on your behalf?

I have to admit to you that patience is one of my biggest struggles. When I want something or need the answer to something, I am the type of person who wants it and wants it now. Can you relate to that? As you probably know, God just doesn't work that way. I have realized that, when He is going to give us what we need, He does it according to His timing, not our impatience.

I look back on my life, and I see that, whenever I tried to make something happen, it just never quite worked out the way I planned. There have been times that I have prayed. . . hard. . . for something to happen, but it didn't. Or maybe it did; just not the way I hoped it would. However, when I waited on God to open a door—or in some cases, close a door—it always seemed to go right. Remember that old song by Garth Brooks; "Unanswered Prayers"? Sometimes, you look back at things you used to pray for and realize how thankful you are that God *didn't* give you what you thought you wanted. And it encourages me to see now what I could not see back then; that God had me safely in His hands the whole time. Whether He was protecting me from certain relationships or guiding me in decisions or through life-changing situations, there has always been a sense that God has a plan for my life, just as I know He does for yours. My favorite Bible verse is this: "'For I know the plans I have for you,' declares the Lord, 'plans to prosper you and not to harm you, plans to give you hope and a future'" (Jeremiah 29:11). When I feel down, or it looks like my plans aren't working out, that verse comes to my mind. It always encourages me, as I hope it does for you too. I hope you know that God has His best in mind for you. What a comfort it is to know this, and more importantly, to believe it's true.

Now, remember when I talked about unanswered prayers earlier? Well, God does answer, just not always the way we plan. What would happen if we prayed and believed for something that wasn't God's best for us? Would He allow it even if it wasn't His perfect will for us? After all, the Bible tells us to "take delight in the Lord, and he will give you the desires of your heart" (Psalm 37:4). God gives us freedom of choice, but what happens when our heart isn't quite right? I wonder, sometimes, if our pain isn't self-inflicted. And if it is, I wonder if there is a lesson to be learned in our pain. I believe God has allowed things to happen in my life so I would learn important lessons He wanted to teach me. With this in mind, I wonder if the most important lesson is to know and understand that God has "plans to prosper you and not to harm you, plans to give you hope and a future" (Jeremiah 29:11). And I wonder if the most important response is to pray "not my will, but yours be done" (Luke 22:42).

So I encourage you today to learn and respond.

BREATHE: Words to Impact Your Prayers

Acknowledge and Admit:

Lord, You are the God who speaks; sometimes, through unanswered prayers.

I tend to need reminding that You are God and I am not.

Appreciate and Ask:

Thank You for protecting me from my own prayers which could have harmed me.

I ask You to help me pray, "Not my will, but Yours be done."

LAP 30

ENDURE TRIALS

FOCUS: Words to Prepare Your Mind

"Anything is possible. This outlook gives us the capacity to dream big, dare to try new things, and believe we can overcome detours and obstacles that get in our way or hold us back."

- Luci Swindoll, A Grand New Day

"Consider it pure joy, my brothers and sisters, whenever you face trials of many kinds, because you know that the testing of your faith produces perseverance"

(James 1:2-3).

PUSH: Words to Influence Your Spirit

Have you been going through a tough couple of days, or maybe even a difficult season of trials in your life?

It may be a financial situation, a sickness, a broken marriage—whatever it may be that you are facing today—let me say that there is light at the end of the darkness you might be experiencing. It's just like the verse above says, "Consider it pure joy, my brothers and sisters, whenever you face trials of many kinds" (James 1:2). Yes, I know it's challenging to think about having joy during rough times, but I want to make you aware that God might be testing your faith. Remember that, through that testing—as the Bible also says, "[I am] confident of this, that he who began a good work in you will carry it on to completion until the day of Christ Jesus" (Philippians 1:6)—He is developing perseverance in you to make you mature and complete, not lacking anything. This is why you can be encouraged during tough times.

There was a season in my life that had been a real challenge physically, mentally, spiritually, and emotionally. Have you ever felt like God has allowed you to go through so many different trials that you feel as though He isn't really there? I don't want you to be discouraged because God is always there and will never leave your side. One of the reasons I say this to you is that, during that season of trials, I felt like I was to go ahead and pursue a career. Well, if I would have known what I was going to experience, I might not have done it. Yet, I felt God told me it was okay. . . but He never said it was going to be easy. Things were going well—so I thought—but little did I know that everything I would put my hand to would seem to fall apart right in front of my eyes. I continued to ask God why. I'm not sure about you, but it takes a lot to get my attention, and boy, does God know how to get it.

"Lord, I thought you told me to go ahead and pursue this career."

At that very moment, I felt as though He said to me, "I did. But I want you to want Me as much as you want these deals to work out. I never said there weren't going to be some challenges along the way. I want to see how much you trust Me, but I continue to see your priorities go by the wayside. So I got your attention by bringing you back to what is most important, and that is Me. No job or desire could ever fulfill you as much as I do. When you focus on Me, I will give you the peace you desire as well as take care of all your needs. So, put all your trust in Me, and only Me and I will give you rest."

When God made that clear to me, I knew He was there. Even though He told me to pursue something, and it was not going as smoothly as I thought, I still thank Him for bringing me back when He saw I was getting off-track. Looking back to that place in my life, I have learned from it and continue to grow from it every day. I am aware much more quickly now when it seems that God is trying to get my attention. Very often, we don't know why God allows certain things to happen or why He allows us to face the trials that we face. However, we cannot forget that God is on our side. He is working behind the scenes on our behalf even if it might not seem like it. He sees the road ahead of us. I firmly believe that He will continue to allow less-than-perfect circumstances to happen until we get what He is trying to teach us. He will allow things to continue to make something that wasn't so good into something great for us and others around us.

So I encourage you today to look at the trials in your life as opportunities for growth. Thank God for His promise to be with you in the hard times. Ask Him to help give you the strength and endurance through these challenges. Then, be patient and allow God to act. As strange as it may seem, we can thank Him for our trials when what we want most of all is to see His will to be done. He will never leave you alone. He will guide and direct you, and more importantly, He will stay close to you and help you grow.

BREATHE: Words to Impact Your Prayers

Acknowledge and Admit:

Lord, You are the reason I can experience joy while I am in the middle of tough times.

I don't like the idea of having my faith tested.

Appreciate and Ask:

Thank You for producing something good (perseverance) from something bad (my trials).

I ask You to help me see my circumstances from Your perspective.

LAP 31

DEVELOP PERSEVERANCE

FOCUS: Words to Prepare Your Mind

"I rely on God's promise to consistently guide me toward fulfilling the purpose for which He created me."

- Luci Swindoll, Imagine Devotional Journal

"Let perseverance finish its work so that you may be mature and complete, not lacking anything"

(James 1:4).

PUSH: Words to Influence Your Spirit

When was the last time it felt like nothing was going right, like you were being tested in every area of your life at the same time, and everything inside you just wanted to give up?

I am going to make some wild statements—wild but true. God has bigger plans for you. Look at your trials as pure blessings because a victory is right around the corner. God is right there beside you, every step of the way. Wasn't He the one who said, "Truly I tell you, if you have faith as small as a mustard seed, you can say to this mountain, 'Move from here to there,' and it will move. Nothing will be impossible for you" (Matthew 17:20). Stand strong. Don't let Satan take your power away.

Every time we feel like giving up, we become a target. Satan tries to come in and kill, steal, and destroy our happiness. We must stand firm in our faith. God promised to carry us through our storms.

There have been many times when I felt like giving up. And just when I started to turn my negative thoughts around toward God's thoughts, He just turned things around for the better. As our thoughts and actions begin to change, this is where God can come in and do His work in us. And that is when we start to have hope. The Bible says, "Keep your lives free from the love of money and be content with what you have, because God has said, 'Never will I leave you; never will I forsake you'" (Hebrews 13:5).

I believe that, at times, God allows us to be tested to see how strong our faith is. I remember a specific time when I wanted an answer to something very badly, but, instead of worrying about it, I prayed and went on a fast with God. I waited for about a month, and during that time, I felt as God told me to "hang in there, be still, and be patient." During that time of earnestly praying to God, I felt that He gave me a clear answer that I was to do nothing until a certain date and that everything would become clear during that time of waiting. I waited and was obedient to what God had asked me to do. And sure enough, the answer came on that very specific date. Whether or not it was the answer I wanted didn't matter because it was God's answer. It can be such a huge faith-builder for us to know that, when we are obedient to what God asks of us, He will always come through. He is faithful even when we are not. And that gives us such a confirmation of *hope*.

So no matter what is going on in your life which may have you feeling like giving up, don't give in to Satan's lies. *God is a God of hope!* When I go through these times—we all do at one time or another—I reflect back on my life and realize that God has never failed me. Do you feel that God has failed you? He might have allowed things to happen that we do not like or situations to come out differently than we thought they would, but thankfully, He has not failed us. God operates on His own timetable. And that is a blessing for us, even though it might not seem that great sometimes. However, because God sees the outcome and what the future holds for us, we really are blessed to have things happen in His time and not ours.

So I encourage you today to look out for the times when you feel like letting go. Just hold on because God is molding you and preparing you for His plan and purpose. He has your best in mind. Keep your spirits high today, and persevere. Don't give up because God will never give up on you.

BREATHE: Words to Impact Your Prayers

Acknowledge and Admit:

Lord, You are always at work in my life, never giving up.

I sometimes fall for the tricks of the enemy and give in.

Appreciate and Ask:

*Thank You for Your unending commitment to me.
Thank You for Your faithfulness.*

I ask You to encourage and strengthen me through Your Word and Your Spirit.

LAP 32

BE CONTENT

FOCUS: Words to Prepare Your Mind

"Celebrate the significance and wonder of life. Don't wait until it hits you over the head. It's already there; waiting for you to embrace it."

- Nicole Johnson, Imagine Devotional Journal

*"I know how to live on almost nothing or with everything.
I have learned the secret of living in every situation, whether
it is with a full stomach or empty, with plenty or little"*

(Philippians 4:12 NLT).

PUSH: Words to Influence Your Spirit

Have you found contentment right where you are in life today or are you still searching for what could make you feel content?

God created us in His image, which is *perfect*. But some of the bad choices we have made since then have created the imperfections that we don't like to see in ourselves. So maybe I should ask if you are content with what you have found to help you *feel* content. We all want to know those kinds of secrets. *How did you get those results? What extra special thing did you find to help?* The bottom line is; there is no magical anything out there that will help us be content. Sure, there may be temporary quick-fixes. However, we find real contentment in knowing Jesus Christ as our Lord and Savior and being thankful for what He has recreated in us.

I look back on my life, and it always seemed as though I was always searching for more. Maybe I would be content with my life if I had more money, more clothes, more this, more that, you fill in the blanks. What I have found that the world's view of contentment—if you have more of the fill-in-the-blank, you will be happy—is temporary, but joy comes from the Lord. Have you ever thought about this; if all those "things" you have in your life were someday taken away, would you still be content? I have found that the more I have, the more I want. However, I have also found that the less I have, the more I find contentment in the little things.

You know that saying "less is more"? Well, I am starting to believe that to be true in my own life. Don't get me wrong. I enjoy the things I have. It's not a bad thing to have or desire things, but I have found that what God wants is for us to find our contentment in Him first, not in "things."

I have been on a fast with God this past month, and I will tell you that God has truly been with me in so many ways. He is incredibly faithful. God has provided even more than what I had lost in sales just a couple of months ago. I have seen more business this month than I have in a long time. And my faith has grown so much stronger. Not only did God provide in my business, but I thrilled to see a good friend's husband receive Jesus. I now have a clearer picture of the direction God is leading me in my ministry. And God did so much more. He is amazing.

When you seek Him first, everything else just seems to follow right along with His plan. A true measurement of happiness or contentment is found in God's love and doing His will. You will find true happiness if you put God above earthly riches. Happiness is temporary, but lasting joy comes from knowing Him.

So I encourage you today to find contentment, not just in the earthly things, but the things which are eternal. Until you find contentment in God first, you will always struggle to find contentment in your life. Look to the things above. That is where the peace of God will continually come upon you from.

BREATHE: Words to Impact Your Prayers

Acknowledge and Admit:

Lord, You are everything I could possibly need.

I am tired of looking for peace and contentment in things that only last for a quick moment.

Appreciate and Ask:

Thank You for offering me a settled heart and a satisfied mind in Jesus.

I ask You to help me stay mindful that all of life's quick-fixes are empty and unfulfilling.

LAP 33

GOD FULFILLS OUR DESIRES

FOCUS: Words to Prepare Your Mind

"Those who desire to live in God's presence each day will be able to enjoy that relationship forever."

- Kimberly Patterson, The Morning Do!: Discovering the Do in You

"Take delight in the Lord, and He will give you the desires of your heart"

(Psalm 37:4).

PUSH: Words to Influence Your Spirit

Are you familiar with what the phrase 'to delight in' means?

You have heard the words of Psalm 37:4 several times during these laps. 'To delight yourself in someone' means to experience great pleasure and joy in his or her presence. If we are going to "delight in the Lord," we must know Him better. If we are going to know him better, we must commit ourselves to Him. This means entrusting everything to His complete control and guidance: our lives, our families, our jobs, our possessions, everything. Committing ourselves to Him means putting our trust in Him and believing that He can care for us better than we ourselves. We must be willing to be patient while we wait for Him to act, and know in our hearts that He knows what is best for us.

Have you ever had a desire in your heart for something or someone so strong that it takes control of your mind? Maybe it is something you want to accomplish in life. Whatever it may be, it can take the most prominent place in our lives and become an idol. So, what are your desires today? God has been making me aware of the desires that are in my heart. I will admit that, at times, they are not always godly desires. My selfish flesh sometimes gets in the way.

When I have a goal to do something or have something, I will do everything in my power to make it happen, almost to the point that everything else around me seems to disappear. I don't do that intentionally, but sometimes it just happens. God knows me—He knows you too—and He knows that it can take a lot to get my attention. So, when it seems as though He has stopped working on my behalf in the area of my number one desire—when no matter what I try, I just cannot seem to gain any ground—He has my attention.

Let me give you a specific example. One of my desires is to be financially debt-free. I know that God wants us to be free of financial bondage, especially when those chains take our focus away from "the Lord who provides." When it comes to bringing our desires to fruition, I truly believe the choices we make along the way will determine the results that we achieve. However, when we put desires and other things above God, He has a way of getting our attention and bringing us back to realizing what is most important. Just to clarify; in this instance, being debt-free is a good thing—something God wants—until I put it ahead of Him in my priorities. That is when it becomes a problem. Do you remember God's commandment "You shall have no other gods before me" (Exodus 20:3)? There are times when I have to ask myself, "Am I doing that?" Am I putting my debt-freedom, or whatever desire it may be that is in my heart, in place of God? When I find myself working too hard to relieve myself of the stress that comes with my burdens, the answer becomes obvious.

There are times when it feels like everything is backfiring on me, to the point that nothing seems to be working in that area of my life. My career, for example, is what makes it possible for me to make money and pay toward the debt that I desire to be free from. And when my career doesn't seem to be working out the way I want it to, I keep hearing a small voice inside of me saying, "Trust Me. I am here for you. When you make Me the deepest desire of your heart, I will provide all of your needs and everything else will fall into place." As I look back on my life and my struggles, I see that, when put God above my own desires and wants, everything does indeed seem to fall into place. Yes, He has always provided for what I need at just the right time.

While on one of my fasts with God, He blessed me in many different ways. One of the blessings came through a retirement fund I had invested in and then forgot about. The company I was with had stopped providing this benefit a few years before. So, at the very time I needed it for my taxes, the company made a payout of the money they owed me. The miracle was in the fact that the funds I was getting were the exact amount I needed.

So I encourage you today to not put people or things like earthly possessions and achievements in God's place. People and things will always let you down, but Jesus never will. Sara Young, in her *Jesus Calling* devotional, says, "Make God your God. Seek His face, and you will find the fulfillment of your deepest longings." I have also found this to be true.

BREATHE: Words to Impact Your Prayers

Acknowledge and Admit:

Lord, You are the One I enjoy, the One I delight in.

I tend to lose my focus and "delight in" things You do for me rather than delighting in You personally.

Appreciate and Ask:

Thank You for Your constant love for me.

I ask You to help me become someone You can delight in.

LAP 34

LAUGH MORE

FOCUS: Words to Prepare Your Mind

"True joy comes only from giving life away—not from striving to keep it."
- Unknown

"A cheerful heart is good medicine"
(Proverbs 17:22).

PUSH: Words to Influence Your Spirit

When was the last time you laughed—I mean the kind of laughter that almost instantly takes away the stress of life? At the very least, the kind of laughter that makes your day a little brighter?

It's not only in happy, feel-good times that we need to laugh. Sometimes, maybe even most of the time, it's when we are in an argument with someone, or when we are overwhelmed by stress and worry. I don't know why it is, but I'm sure you would agree; things lighten up a bit when we laugh. Tension begins to melt. Laughter is refreshing. They say that laughter is good for the soul. I believe we all need more laughter in our lives. We just don't laugh enough. I know there are times when I could use a little more laughter. I believe that God wants us to enjoy life to its fullest and laugh. A lot. However, it seems as though high-stress levels in our everyday life keep us from doing that.

Do children laugh a lot? Do they have fun? Enjoy life? We all know that most of them do. Now, let's take a moment and remember when we were a little girl or boy. Let's ask ourselves, *What happened to the little child inside of me? Why don't I laugh, or even smile, enough? Why do I worry about little things that don't even matter?* It's a matter of redirecting our thinking, isn't it? Even though we don't live in the body of a child anymore, the child within us is still there. God wants us to be more childlike in our faith. He wants us to enjoy life, and to resist worrying and taking on the full weight of our burdens. He wants us to "cast all [our] anxiety on Him because he cares for [us]" (1 Peter 5:7). He can lighten the load we carry.

So I encourage you today to know that God is right there with you, with open arms, asking you to let Him carry you through this. "Come to me, all you who are weary and burdened, and I will give you rest" (Matthew 11:28). I challenge you today to let the weight of your burdens go. Try, and give it to God. You might find yourself laughing more. You might find joy in your life again. Bring out the child inside you, who wants to play, and enjoy everything that God has created you to be. The title of that book by Richard Carlson it is so true—*Don't Sweat the Small Stuff*. Life is too short. We have to make every day count, so *live fully*, *laugh often*, and *love more*!

BREATHE: Words to Impact Your Prayers

Acknowledge and Admit:

Lord, You are the One who brings cheerfulness to my heart.

I tend to take things too seriously sometimes.

Appreciate and Ask:

Thank You for offering me a life of joy and happiness and laughter.

I ask You to help me make a proper place in my life for light-heartedness.

LAP 35

LIVE JOYFULLY

FOCUS: Words to Prepare Your Mind

*"Joy is prayer; joy is strength: joy is love;
joy is a net of love by which you can catch souls."*

- Mother Teresa

*"Rejoice in the Lord always. I will say it again: Rejoice!
Let your gentleness be evident to all. The Lord is near"*

(Philippians 4:4-5).

PUSH: Words to Influence Your Spirit

Are you overflowing with joy today, or are you letting someone or something steal your joy from you?

God wants us to experience a life full of joy. I have found that the key to having complete joy in my life is having a consistent relationship with Jesus Christ. Yes, I said 'consistent'! What does that look like for me? It means that I pray, read the Bible, and connect with Jesus every day, whether it's for 5 minutes, 30 minutes, or much longer. God wants our time and attention focused on Him, whatever that might look like for us.

In my everyday life, I can get so busy with juggling work and kids and various challenges that come my way. I'm sure you can relate to that. I find that, if I don't spend time with Jesus every day, my life is so much more hectic, which leaves an open door for Satan to come in and take away my joy. However, when I make time for God every day, my life is so much more complete. Jesus said, "I have told you this so that my joy may be in you and that your joy may be complete" (John 15:11). It is the joy of living with Jesus Christ daily which will keep us level-headed no matter how high or how low our circumstances.

So I encourage you today to be consistent with talking to Jesus on a daily basis. He hears you. It is just a matter of slowing down and listening to what God says to you. This verse stood out to me when I read it long ago, and I have always remembered it; "Therefore my heart is glad and my tongue rejoices; my body also will rest secure" (Psalm 16:9). Happiness is temporary because it is based on external circumstances that can change. However, joy is lasting. We can feel joy in spite of our deepest troubles because it is based on God's presence within us. So as you contemplate His daily presence, you will find contentment. You will experience joy as you begin to understand the future He has in store for you. Don't base your life on circumstances but on God.

BREATHE: Words to Impact Your Prayers

Acknowledge and Admit:

Lord, You are the source of eternal joy.

I often find it easier to be joking instead of joyful.

Appreciate and Ask:

Thank You for the lasting joy that comes from salvation and my relationship with You.

I ask You to make Your presence known to me daily so that my joy will be continuous.

ON A FAST TRACK WITH GOD

HOME STRETCH

*"Do you not know that in a race all the runners run,
but only one gets the prize? Run in such a way as to get the prize"*

(1 Corinthians 9:24).

LAP 36

IS GOD CALLING YOU?

FOCUS: Words to Prepare Your Mind

"God can do more than you ever imagined, but to embrace all God wants you to do you must walk in faithfulness."

- Sarah Young, Jesus Calling

"I am the vine; you are the branches. If you remain in Me and I in you, you will bear much fruit; apart from Me, you can do nothing"

(John 15:5).

PUSH: Words to Influence Your Spirit

What would you do if it felt like God was leading you in a specific direction; like He was calling you to do something?

I truly believe that when God calls us to do things for Him, He does not give up until His plan is fulfilled. In my experience, it sometimes seems that it is taking a long time for God's plan to be fulfilled—you might feel the same way too. However, I wonder if we sometimes get in the way of the plan. What I mean is this; we seem to get ourselves so busy in our everyday lives that God doesn't have much of a chance to teach us or complete the work He wants to do in us. We don't slow down and focus enough to allow Him to work in the ways He wants to. As His plan unfolds, He wants us to learn lessons through all of it. This is why we need to keep our eyes focused on Him. God did not 'halfway' create us; He doesn't want to do things in our lives 'halfway' either. When He does anything, He does it perfectly. He will not give up. He makes sure the work He is doing is what we need and just when we need it. His timing is perfect! God will not cheat us out of anything He knows would be the very best for us.

God called me to write the very book in your hands a few years back. I had always told myself that I am not a writer, but God must have seen me differently. I became convinced of His calling the day something quite dramatic happened. I had been working on my notes and earliest writings, off and on, for some time. One day, I knew that God was prompting me to continue my writing when I realized I had lost the rough draft of my book. I found myself between the panic of "God asked me to write this" and the flimsy excuse of "I am not a writer." *Okay, God. If You truly want me to write this book, I need You to help me find it.* I had no clue whatsoever as to where it could have been. A few days later, a little brown box in the garage caught my attention. It was sitting right next to the trash can. You can already guess what was inside; the rough draft of this book. I found a mission from God that day, figuratively speaking, between 'trash day' and a second chance. We often find God's plan for us there. God had made His point very clear. I was to continue writing this book, despite my insecurities about it. He obviously has a plan for what He wants to accomplish with it—which may very well include you—so I decided to be obedient and finish it just as He asked me to. I learned that, even with self-doubts about being a writer, when God works right beside me and through me, I can do anything.

I cannot say it strongly enough; when God has a plan for your life, He will make it possible for you to succeed in fulfilling it. Remember; anything is possible with God. Don't doubt for one second that He can do something through you. Open your heart and trust Him. "In their hearts humans plan their course, but the Lord establishes their steps" (Proverbs 16:9). "He who began a good work in you will carry it on to completion" (Philippians 1:6).

In her devotional *Jesus Calling*, Sarah Young writes this from the Lord's heart to yours; "Take time to be still in My presence so that I can strengthen you. The busier you become, the more you need this time apart with Me."

So I encourage you today to always move toward God's plan. When He lays something specific on your heart, He does it for a reason. Don't ignore it. If what is in your heart is His plan for you, He will lead you in the direction you should go. If not, He will turn you in a direction that He knows will be best for you. The most important thing about this is keeping your heart open to His plan. Trust Him. Know that He is leading you with a plan and a purpose.

BREATHE: Words to Impact Your Prayers

Acknowledge and Admit:

Lord, You are the God who calls me to serve You.

*I need You to convince me of Your calling
when it is much bigger than I can see.*

Appreciate and Ask:

Thank You for inviting me to be a part of Your work on the earth.

*I ask You to lead my 'everyday life' as well as
my work for Your kingdom.*

LAP 37

WAITING ON GOD

FOCUS: Words to Prepare Your Mind

"We need to focus on the wonder of God's plan, His vision for our lives, and the marvelous pictures of God's purpose for a woman's life."

- Sheila Walsh, Imagine Devotional Journal

"Do not be anxious about anything, but in every situation, by prayer and petition, with thanksgiving, present your requests to God. And the peace of God, which transcends all understanding, will guard your hearts and your minds in Christ Jesus."

(Philippians 4:6-7)

PUSH: Words to Influence Your Spirit

How well can you wait on God?

You may remember that on our 29th lap together, we talked about the need for us to learn patience. During this lap and the next two, I am going to revisit the subject of waiting on God. I hope to take it in a direction that could help prepare you for a specific work God has for you to do in life.

So, I ask again; how well can you wait on God?

When we feel we need an answer right away, it can seem as if God is taking an especially long time. I know it can be very difficult for me to wait on Him because, when I want something to happen, I want it to happen 'now.' Do you struggle with this too? God doesn't always answer us immediately, but what He does do is answer us at the right time. God's time is always the perfect time. As I look back on my life, I see that He has always answered in some way. It may not have been "my way," but He answered. I believe—and I know you will feel the same—that He has never failed me. He has always been there when I needed Him most. Let me tell you; even if everything else around you fails, God never will. The Bible says that "Jesus Christ is the same yesterday and today and forever" (Hebrews 13:8).

I believe that, when we are waiting for God to give us an answer or do something on our behalf, He is watching to see how completely we put our trust in Him. He wants us to learn and grow during our waiting periods. We have a choice. We can wallow in our waiting and feel sorry for ourselves because God is not doing *what* we want *when* we want, or we can be patient. We can believe that God knows what's best for us. We can expect that He will provide for us and give us answers that are best for us in the long run. God sees our future. He knows what lies ahead for us. Even though we don't know what may be coming next, it is a beautiful thing to be at peace, knowing that everything is in God's trustworthy hands. When we trust Him, when we believe He is there for us and sees the road ahead, we can continue to move forward in life. We can make the most of the time we have. He wants to show us something powerful, something which will empower us. We can be thankful to Him while we wait. If we wallow in pity, we may very well miss out on what God is trying to show us. Instead, when we are waiting on God, we should just be still and listen, and rest assured that God is God. He sees what is ahead for us and wants the absolute best for us. I am telling you now to wait in peace because the God who loves you already knows the outcome.

I once fasted and prayed for a year and a half that a specific deal would close, and after that long wait, it finally did. I am convinced that it was worth every bit of the waiting because of the lessons God taught me during that time. They were so much greater than I could have ever imagined at the beginning of the process. My faith in Him grew by leaps and bounds.

So as we end this lap together—with the finish line ahead—I encourage you today that, although it may feel as though God is taking a long time to answer your prayer, don't give up. There are things happening in the meantime that you should pay attention to. God is doing much more than 'making you wait.' Look for what it is He may be doing.

Even if the wait takes a year and a half, or ten times longer, "know that in all things God works for the good of those who love Him, who have been called according to His purpose" (Romans 8:28).

BREATHE: Words to Impact Your Prayers

Acknowledge and Admit:

Lord, You are deliberate about the work You do in my life.

*I tend to not be very patient as You mold me
into the likeness of Jesus.*

Appreciate and Ask:

Thank You for the work You do in my life every day, even when I don't see it.

I ask You to help me be patient as You bring about exactly what is in Your heart for me.

LAP 38

RIGHT THING AT THE WRONG TIME

FOCUS: Words to Prepare Your Mind

"God tells us that He knew us in our mother's womb. He tells us that He knows us, even better than we know ourselves. And best of all, He knows something beyond what we know; He knows what He is calling us to become."

- Nicole Johnson, Imagine Devotional Journal

"Look at the nations and watch—and be utterly amazed. For I am going to do something in your days that you would not believe, even if you were told"

(Habakkuk 1:5).

PUSH: Words to Influence Your Spirit

What would you do if it felt like God was leading you in a specific direction, but the timing wasn't quite right?

Just recently, God presented my husband and me with an opportunity which seemed to come out of a clear blue sky. Of course, we know where it really came from; *God*. It was a job opportunity and a great one for our family.

I had been fasting, as well as praying together with my husband, for the previous few months for God to show us the direction He wanted us to go in. When the new opportunity came up, our first reaction was to "drop everything and just do it because, *obviously*, this is the right thing to do." Or so we thought. I remember praying and asking God to "please give us a sure sign whether we are to accept the opportunity or not." I felt as though He told me "just wait. Your answer will be very clear."

In the days that followed, my husband shared the situation with close friends in his life, and the feedback he received was quite affirming. Separately, a couple of his friends said the same thing. They believed that God was, first of all, affirming that we are going in the right direction. However, they added, "The timing might not be right yet. God may be preparing you now to take the opportunity later."

Then, God gave us a very clear sign just like He told us He would. He sent someone to my husband directly who told him, "I see you as a person who is qualified to lead in a position like this, but this particular position is not the one that is right for you." Because those words came from a very influential person in our church and in our lives, we knew that was a sign from God. We knew the message could not be any clearer. It was very encouraging to us that God wanted us to know that there was *more* to come, but for now, we should just be still.

Honestly, not all of the answers I have prayed to God about have been this clear. However, on this occasion, we were sure of it, and as enticing as the opportunity seemed to be, God saw the bigger picture of our lives and an opportunity like this one was not meant to be for us at that time.

So I ask you; are you facing anything like this? Do you know that God is leading you in a general direction, yet this may not be the specific time to take the full plunge and go for it? Whether the timing is not quite right or perfect, I want to say to you; *listen* to what God is saying and be *obedient*. I am sure that if you do what He tells you to do—or not to do—He will continue to lead you in the direction you should go. You *will* know His desire for your life. Whether you encounter open doors or closed, following Him will lead to more blessing than you could ever imagine.

So I encourage you today; God puts desires in our heart which He knows we have the ability to accomplish. I truly believe that. So be open to all God has for you. If He wants you to do something, He will continue to bring it up. He will continue to put it in your path until you see it. If you are on God's path—you are going in His direction for your life—but things are not going the way you thought they would, don't worry. God never said the life of a Christian would be easy, but He does ask us to trust Him. Know that He has a plan, not to harm us, but to prosper us. He will never put anything before us that we cannot handle. He will never leave our side. His plan will be carried through to the end.

BREATHE: Words to Impact Your Prayers

Acknowledge and Admit:

Lord, You are the God of timing as well as opportunity.

I need for You to tell me when the opportunity and timing are both right.

Appreciate and Ask:

Thank You for making things clear to me when I come to You with doubts.

I ask You to show me when it is the right thing at the right time.

LAP 39

RIGHT THING AT THE RIGHT TIME

FOCUS: Words to Prepare Your Mind

"A longing is the heart whispering to the mind that we human beings were made for more than this world has to offer us. I believe they are from God."

- Nicole Johnson, Imagine Devotional Journal

"Once more I will astound these people with wonder upon wonder; the wisdom of the wise will perish, the intelligence of the intelligent will vanish"

(Isaiah 29:14).

PUSH: Words to Influence Your Spirit

What would you do if it felt like God was calling you to do something and that the time is *now*?

There are many times in our lives when it is important to not make a quick decision but to wait on God to give us the answer we seek. I truly believe, however, that there are also times when the answer is obvious and immediate. It is right there in the middle of an unexpected moment. Sometimes, God puts certain situations and people in front of us at the exact, right time. How well do we trust Him and respond in those moments?

One morning, my young son and I were laughing and having fun together, and he wanted me to read to him. He often joined me in my devotional time and enjoyed it when I read out loud. This morning was no different. We were reading that day's devotional thought when he turned to me suddenly and asked me if he was going to heaven when he died. I could have dismissed the seriousness of his question. After all, some might say that a child that young certainly doesn't understand the theological concepts involved. Of course, many grownups have trouble comprehending the fragility of life and the urgency of faith as well. However, I had a knowing that God was giving me a legitimate opportunity to share with him about Jesus. It is recorded in three of the four gospels that Jesus said, "Let the little children come to Me, and do not hinder them, for the kingdom of heaven belongs to such as these" (Matthew 19:14; also Mark 10:14 and Luke 18:16). I told my son that, to go to heaven, you have to ask Jesus into your heart. "Would you like to do that?"

He nodded and said, "Yes, mommy."

As a mom, I was very excited to take the opportunity I had been presented. As I prayed, he repeated my prayer and accepted Jesus into his heart. It was precious, tender moment. Tears were streaming down my face. I cannot describe the joy of discovering that my young son already had a desire to learn more about Jesus. It was such a blessing to experience that with him.

So I encourage you today; if God is putting an opportunity right in front of you, especially if it is an opportunity to bless, expand and strengthen His kingdom, don't wait. Make the most of that moment. Even though I knew that my little son did not understand everything completely, I knew it was a moment to help him begin to know about God. His age did not matter because God was right there in the moment. He was guiding that opportunity. I could see my son's heart and tell that he was taking it in as sincerely as he was able to. My perspective has always been that, if there is an opportunity for me to lead someone to Christ, I am not going to pass it up. Sometimes, the opportunity in front of you is the only time you will have to make a difference in that person's life. Whatever opportunities or decisions you face, whether big or small, when God gives you peace that the time is now, go for it. Don't wait!

BREATHE: Words to Impact Your Prayers

Acknowledge and Admit:

Lord, You are the One who offers me divine appointments and perfect timing.

I am not always aware of eternal moments that might be right in front of me.

Appreciate and Ask:

Thank You for the nudges You give me when the time is right.

*I ask You to help me see all of the opportunities
I have to make a difference in people's lives.*

ON A FAST TRACK WITH GOD

FINISH LINE

*"I have fought the good fight,
I have finished the race,
I have kept the faith"*

(2 Timothy 4:7).

LAP 40

HOPE AND A FUTURE

FOCUS: Words to Prepare Your Mind

"The more you put your hope in God the more God's love shines upon you brightening your day."

- Sarah Young, Jesus Calling

"We wait in hope for the Lord; He is our help and our shield. In Him our hearts rejoice, for we trust in His holy name. May Your unfailing love be with us, Lord, even as we put our hope in You"

(Psalm 33:20-22).

PUSH: Words to Influence Your Spirit

What was the most important thing you gained from running these 40 laps with me? Was there a specific *a-ha* moment with God?

As we run this 40th and final lap together, I want you to know how proud I am of you. I believe that God is proud of you as well for completing these 40 daily devotions. It really doesn't matter how long it took for you to cross the finish line; 40 days or 400. You are here now; it is never too late to finish strong.

It took four years for this non-writer to write the devotional book in your hands. For me, the most important thing was not finding the perfect words for every page, but rather to authentically share stories and lessons from my times of fasting. God called me to write them down. I was obedient to His call. I finished the work He gave me to do. I think of Paul's words to Timothy, his partner in the ministry; "I have fought the good fight, I have finished the race, I have kept the faith" (2 Timothy 4:7). Now that is what I call 'finishing strong.'

I prayed for you a lot while I wrote this devotional. One of the things I prayed was that you would find more hope in your life. Just remember; no matter what kind of difficult time you may face today or any day in the future, if you have God, you have hope because God *is* hope! He has a plan and a purpose for your life. You have so much to look forward to. Believe that. Receive it!

I can only speak for myself, of course, but as I have said, fasting has always been one of the best faith-builders in my life. I would pray that you would begin fasting or continue to fast, as God calls you to do so. He can do the impossible. Don't doubt Him for a minute. You don't always have to fast for 40 days like I do. If you are just starting, or you just want some clarity and peace about something in your life, a 1-day or 3-day fast can be good. The number of days doesn't matter much because God knows your heart and He wants to bless you beyond measure. I do suggest that, if you need a new start to life, 40 days can make for a great 'new beginning.' After all, they say that it takes 21 days to break a habit. Forty days can not only break the bad ones but also establish some good, godly habits in your life.

So, my friend, I sincerely pray for you today; I ask God to bless you and keep you as you continue on this journey of life that He has called you to. Always remember; "God is able to bless you abundantly, so that in all things at all times, having all that you need, you will abound in every good work." (2 Corinthians 9:8).

BREATHE: Words to Impact Your Prayers

Acknowledge and Admit:

Lord, You are the God of hope.
You have a plan and a purpose for my life.

My hope sometimes wavers when I face difficult days.

Appreciate and Ask:

Thank You for blessing me abundantly so I can do Your good work.

I ask You to help me value the discipline of fasting
as I truly dedicate myself to You.

ACKNOWLEDGEMENTS

I feel so blessed to have been able to write this devotional. I could not have done it alone, and I would like to thank some very valuable people in my life who have helped me along the journey.

I want to thank, first and foremost, Jesus, my Lord and Savior, for giving me the strength and the courage to write this devotional. He kept me going—persevering through the challenges—even when I couldn't believe it was possible to do this.

I want to thank my amazing husband, Bryan, and my two kids, Kylee and Joshua, for always believing in me and supporting me through this process.

I also want to thank my mom, Nancy, for raising me in a home of Christian values and always telling me that there is power in the name of Jesus, and my dad, Steve, for always letting me know that I can do anything that I set my mind to do.

Thank you to my Aunt Carol who wrote the Foreword of this book. She inspired me to incorporate fasting into my life as a form of worshipping Jesus. She encouraged my very first 40 days of fasting!

Thank you to Clint Sprague, the pastor of our church, and the *Women of Faith* organization for inspiring me with their insights and wisdom.

And finally, thank you to my wonderful editor, Eric Holmes, who made this book come to life.